FROM MORNING 'TIL NIGHT:

PERSPECTIVES ON ADHD AND ITS MANAGEMENT

Frances C. Sutherland, PhD

with illustrations by Bob Perkins

ISBN 978-1-7320341-0-5

Printed in the United States of America

While this book covers important aspects of ADHD, it is not intended to be a substitute for the evaluation and treatment of the condition by medical and/or mental health professionals. Although every effort has been made to provide accurate information, the author is not responsible for any errors, omissions or conclusions drawn from the information presented. Readers are encouraged to seek out additional sources of information to confirm or refute the contents of this book.

Contact Information
fsutherland233@gmail.com
BobPerkinsDrawsThings@gmail.com
www.bob-perkins.com/

With thanks to all the families in my practice who have taught me so much and with love and gratitude to my family, Matt, Carrie and Bill.

FCS

For Mom, Dad, Nicole, my grandparents (Thomas & Cecelia Betson and Robert & Lois Perkins) and my mentor, Marion Kassab, all of whom never gave up on me.

BP

CONTENTS

Author's Note	The Reason for this Book:	7
	Turning unease into action	
Chapter 1	Open to the Public:	11
	Making ADHD more accessible	
Chapter 2	Essential Theory about ADHD:	18
	What you really need to know	
Chapter 3	ADHD and Behavior Change:	36
	Much more complicated than you might think	
Chapter 4	ADHD and Family Dynamics:	57
	Ready or not, everybody's impacted	
Chapter 5	Patients' Perspectives on Medication:	67
	What it does and does not provide	
Chapter 6	Pulling It All Together	77
	Acknowledgments	80
	Appendices	82
	References	86
	List of Resources	90
	About the Authors	91

AUTHOR'S NOTE
The Reason for this Book:
Turning unease into action

My unease began in late January 2012 with the article "Ritalin Gone Wrong" in the Sunday Review of *The New York Times*. My discomfort gathered steam throughout the year with a steady output of front page articles about stimulant misuse in the management of Attention Deficit/Hyperactivity Disorder (ADHD).[1] Over time in my day-to-day psychotherapy practice, I saw a confirmation emerge of others' unease as well, expressed in various forms: disbelief and distress from my adolescent and adult patients and their family members; concern and upset from my fellow mental health professionals; and inquiries from friends and family members who knew that I specialized in the treatment of ADHD and learning disabilities. Finally, I decided, my growing discomfort needed to be addressed.

I pushed myself to define my unease. What was it exactly? I realized that it was a profound sense of disconnect between what was being presented to the public about the nature and management of ADHD and the reality of what I did every day in my office. To be sure, the condition is very challenging to manage effectively because fundamentally it disrupts ones ability to regulate his or her behavior throughout the day. Left undiagnosed and untreated, individuals with ADHD constantly find themselves at the mercy of what they are thinking and feeling in the moment versus being able to chart out possible courses of action and flexibly execute not only daily plans but also larger life goals.

However problematic the condition, the mounting press coverage had conveyed a picture of ADHD and its management that by turns seemed so bleak, so simplistic and at times, truthfully, so incompetent that I just couldn't stay quiet any longer. I became convinced that the general reader interested in this subject should be getting a more thorough, balanced picture of effective management, as well as a more nuanced, accurate view of the condition and what it means for an individual and his or her family members. Most importantly, I felt that the patients and their families deserved to have a voice in this discussion beyond the characterization of treatment disasters (e.g., suicides, misuse/addiction to stimulants, etc.) being depicted in the press during that period.

With the goal of addressing these inaccuracies and biases, and with encouragement from many quarters, I began the thinking and writing that would result in this book. Initially, this involved some indirect steps. I wrote letters to *The New York Times* in response to some of its articles, including one that became the basis for *The Sunday Dialogue*. This letter writing campaign has continued, with the most recent running in October 2016 in *The New York Times Magazine* in response to a feature article, "Generation Adderall"

---

1   ADHD is an abbreviation referring to all forms of the condition (hyperactive-impulsive, inattentive and combined presentations), and it is the formal, standard term used for diagnosis. See Chapter 1 for more information.

by Casey Schwartz. Also, after 25 years of developing a model of ADHD treatment (The Integrated Model of ADHD Management), I attained copyrights related to the model's interventions. Distilled from the daily operations of my practice and based on my reading and thoughts about ADHD over the years, these writings occupy a central place in this effort.

Before I go any further describing how I decided to write this book, let's pause for a moment. Consider this the "fork in the road" on the Author's Note highway. Those of you who want to start learning about the condition and its management, exit here and go to Chapter 1. For the rest of you who would like to know more about my process and want an overview of the book, stay in your lane and proceed.

Objectives and Overview

My goal was to write a book about ADHD and its management that general interest readers--as patients, parents, educators or interested others--would find engaging, accurate, informative and helpful in managing the condition. To do so, I latched onto the idea of including cartoons to make the theory easier to understand and help readers retain key concepts. I know some of this information can be challenging to grasp, but I am confident that with some persistence and willingness to review, it is within reach.

Another objective was to give readers an accurate overall picture of the condition and key aspects of its management in under 100 pages. As such, within each topic I zero in on core concepts that should permit anyone to apprehend quickly the key information. The book is comprised of six chapters, with the heart of it (i.e., what the condition is and how it is treated) in Chapters 1-4. In keeping with the goal of accuracy with accessibility, treatment of each topic is more targeted than comprehensive. For example, while Chapter 2 deals with the nature of ADHD, it does not cover a wide range of thinking about the condition. Rather, I present a point of view—that ADHD is a disorder of behavior regulation—and support it through my understanding of current theory and research, and my clinical experience.

I also focus exclusively on patients and their families. While other relationships, such as school or friends, can bear on a treatment plan, they only capture fragments of the condition. A patient's parents (and sometimes siblings) are usually the only individuals who have seen the evolution of the condition from its first manifestations through to its current presentation. I believe understanding how ADHD is shaped by family interactions is vital to appreciating both what it is and the magnitude of its potential impact.

The age range of patients was another variable I had to address when considering the book's focus. As the condition is usually diagnosed in middle childhood (i.e., 5-12 years of age), many of the examples pertain specifically to this age group. That said, I have also included examples and comments from adolescents, adults and their family members, most particularly parents. As is the case with any book containing patient information, confidentiality must be protected, and therefore actual names have been changed. And where I am using direct quotes from actual patients, only fictional first names are used.

In addition to comments from patients and their parents, I also created "depictions" of situations that frequently recur in the course of treatment with me. While these "depictions" are fictionalized, they are nonetheless amalgamations of comments and stories I hear about all the time. Their inclusion aims to give the reader the clearest sense possible of the diagnostic concepts or treatment considerations with which individuals and their families grapple on a daily basis. I take a similar approach for issues pertaining to behavior change and family dynamics (Chapters 3 and 4, respectively).

Controversy and heated opinions surround the issue of stimulant medication, and I decided to address it in a somewhat novel way, one that did not make its use the focal point of treatment. As such, medication is not discussed until Chapter 5, near the book's end, for two reasons. First, I wanted readers to think about the role of medication in the management of ADHD only after they had become acquainted with the nature of the condition and two key aspects of its treatment (behavior management and family dynamics).

Sequencing the chapters in this way also permitted patient perspectives to become the primary focus of Chapter 5, and I wanted to showcase the experience of individuals who actually take this medication and use it responsibly. Their perspectives are real, first person accounts of what these drugs do and don't do. They contain views which are rarely articulated in standard patient guides that focus on types of medications, how they work, possible side effects and such. It is my hope that these first-person accounts will be both interesting and informative to general interest readers, but will be particularly valuable to patients contemplating a trial of medication.

My second reason for placing the medication chapter at the end bears on the traditional role that stimulant medication has occupied in the overall management of ADHD. To be sure, it is an important component of treatment, particularly because it lays the foundation for being able to utilize fully other types of management. Too often though in the popular press, medication is the centerpiece of discussions about treatment with issues such as misuse and side effects. Scant if any attention is paid to depictions that provide a more balanced view of medication's true costs and benefits. The popular press also ignores the range of medical treatments, instead focusing on medication. Often psychologists (such as myself) work closely with psychiatrists and other medical professionals to develop and monitor medication protocols (one or more prescription drugs) which address other issues in addition to the patient's ADHD.

Also, and this may come as a surprise to some readers, a major emphasis on medication does not reflect what actually transpires with children, adolescent adults and their families in my office. More commonly, once a medication protocol is up and running and working effectively, relatively little time is devoted to it because to do so would waste valuable treatment time – time that is better spent on sorting out how to manage issues pertaining to behavior change and family dynamics.

Finally, the book attempts to offer a realistic picture of how treatment proceeds, particularly when patients and their families are operating from a shared framework of what the condition is and how to deal with it well. I hope you will see how collaborative and effective management can be and yet begin to appreciate how dispiriting it can be to deal with a condition that persists in disrupting lives in small and large ways, day in and day out. And yet, when families adopt and maintain a collaborative stance with respect to managing the condition, they have found one of the keys to success in managing ADHD. Moreover, getting and staying in a collaborative zone also provides satisfaction and comfort independent of how well or how poorly things are going for an individual (and his/her family) at any given moment.

Topics not addressed

There are a number of important issues I do not attempt to address in this book. In order to focus on the elements I felt were most essential for an understanding of the management of ADHD, I had to leave some things out. Specifically, I elected not to discuss so-called co-morbid conditions (e.g., anxiety and mood disorders, oppositional behavior disorders), nor other neurodevelopmental delays (learning disabilities, autism spectrum disorders), although any interested reader needs to know that co-occurring conditions are frequently part of a patient's profile when ADHD is diagnosed. Likewise, problems with sleep can exacerbate or even masquerade as ADHD (see Vatsal Thakkar's 4/28/2013 article in the *Sunday Review* section of *The New York Times*). Exercise can help to moderate some of the symptoms of ADHD (see John Ratey's book, *Spark: The revolutionary new science of exercise and the brain*). As with co-morbidity, both of these issues are important in management of ADHD, and I urge interested readers to explore the topics using the above references as starting points.

CHAPTER 1
Open to the Public:
Making ADHD more accessible

Harvard Medical School Conferences
OPEN TO THE PUBLIC
Monday - Friday, 9:00 - 12:15 PM
Registration begins at 8:30 AM

Entering the exclusive lobby of the Naples Beach Hotel and Golf Resort, I was struck by a sign for the conference: "Open to the Public." My initial thought was, "Wow, how great."

Apparently everyone was welcome to attend an elite conference for psychiatrists, psychologists, social workers, nurses and other mental health professionals. Brushing aside the practical (and somewhat cynical) reason that Harvard could generate more registration fees, "Open to the Public" quickly shifted in my mind from a plus to more of a paradox. Having attended the same conference two years prior, I knew what was in store: a blue spiral bound book filled with slides, many of them graphs and charts with research study findings, graphic representations of neurons that depicted the release and uptake of neurochemicals and MRI scans of the brain's prefrontal cortex. How could members of the public with little or no background in ADHD walk in and truly engage with the material being presented by the prominent Harvard psychiatrist leading the week-long program?

How indeed? Once again, I found myself confronting the issue of accessibility to accurate information about ADHD and its management – the driving force behind the book in your hands. As is evident from the Author's Note, my experience with news reports and opinion pieces on ADHD had convinced me that the general reader interested in this topic was not being served well by intermittent articles that covered treatment problems (principally with medication) without providing a full picture of what the condition is and what is involved in managing it effectively.

Starting points: Theory and practice in plain language

As would be true of any reputable resource on a medical topic, correctly explaining ADHD and its management is a paramount concern. Added to that challenge is the goal of providing explanations that are also readable and relatively easy to digest. Culling through all the material I could have presented, I stuck with some of the time-honored giants in psychiatry, psychology and mental health (Freud, Skinner, Piaget), as well as major thinkers making contributions in the latter 20th/early 21st centuries (Russell Barkley, Adele Diamond, Salvador Minuchin). By combining their thinking with my perspective and those of my patients and their families, my intention is to provide a balance between theory and practice which permits a clear picture of ADHD to emerge.

Lots of information and just as much misunderstanding

Information about ADHD seems to be everywhere. Sources as varied as the CDC, WebMD, Additude magazine, web sites of pharmaceutical companies, national news broadcasts, and social media all have carried reports on ADHD across a wide variety of topic areas. Prevalence rates, misuse of stimulants, nature of the condition, conventional treatments, alternative treatments, heritability of the condition, and associated problems in social and academic areas are just some of the issues you'll find. And it's not just digital information. Go into any pediatrician office and you will find pamphlets on ADHD sitting along side the hand-outs on asthma and acne.

Education has gotten on board as well. In 2018, primary and secondary school teachers are not only aware of the condition, but in many cases have been trained actively to look out for persistent signs of hyperactivity, impulsivity or inattention, all of which might signal the presence of ADHD.

Yet despite the easy availability of a variety of information about ADHD, I continue to sense that a meaningful and integrated portrayal of the condition is sorely lacking. I became aware of this "understanding gap" in working with my patients and their families, particularly as they came to understand ADHD as a disorder of behavioral regulation which affects one's functioning throughout the day, and as they learned how to bring about behavior change for themselves and their children. One comment from a mother in my practice captured this idea as she talked about her work with Andrew, her 8-year-old with ADHD:

"It really helped me to think about ADHD in terms of what you said--something that affects Andrew from the time he gets up in the morning until he goes to bed at night. Until now I hadn't thought about it as a more constant condition, and I really didn't appreciate just how big an impact it was having on him. Now I see he wasn't really taking in as much of what we were telling him to do as I had thought, so it's understandable why he wasn't changing his behavior in spite of our repeated requests."

Andrew's mother's comment illustrated the understanding gap I had been sensing; but how could I address it?

Making sense of symptoms

Years from now, the voice messages on my service will continue to play back in my mind.

"Dr. Sutherland, my name is Mary Baxter. My son David is a kindergartner at Spring Street Elementary and all year his teacher has been concerned about his 'activity level.' He talks during group instruction and has trouble staying seated. He is having trouble staying focused and completing his daily seat work. At home, he isn't able to occupy himself with toys and has trouble getting along with other children because he always wants to win.

You were referred to us by Dr. Lee, our pediatrician. We are wondering if he has ADHD? He has always had difficulty with activities that involve sitting in a circle and listening to a teacher or an adult. We saw this throughout preschool."

Another variant of this message:

"Hi Dr. Sutherland. My name is Janet Parker. My daughter Melissa is in fourth grade at Meadowlark School. This year and last year, she started having problems producing written work in school and she never wants to study for social studies and science tests. She has always been forgetful and has always wanted us to help with tasks. My husband and I think she should be doing more on her own--picking out her school clothes, getting dressed promptly and leaving the house on time to get the bus. A friend of mine, Laurie Allen, worked with you with her son Charlie and referred me to you. We're wondering if Melissa has attention-deficit disorder, not the hyperactive type, but the more day-dreamy kind."

Over time, the linkages and disparities contained in these two messages shaped my understanding of this condition. Leave aside for a moment whether the adjustment problems presented rise to the level of true ADHD. Simply pay attention to the following points: Both kids are having trouble regulating their behavior in order to meet the demands of their environments at home and at school, and in both cases, these signs of trouble appear to have been present for an extended period of time.

That said, the areas of primary concern are somewhat different for each child. David's difficulties seem to be centered in hyperactivity (trouble staying seated), impulsivity (talking during group instruction) and inattention (trouble focusing in order to finish daily seat work). This triad of problems resembles what mental health practitioners refer to as ADHD, Combined presentation, because the symptoms David is showing include elements of both hyperactivity/impulsivity and inattention. With Melissa, her difficulties--forgetfulness, insufficient independence with self–care, low motivation around test preparation, and trouble producing written work—are consistent with symptoms of ADHD, Predominantly inattentive presentation.[2]

Moving from diagnosis to a fuller understanding of symptoms

Let's assume that the diagnostic evaluations for David and Melissa were each confirmed and we are moving on to treatment. How would I begin? The first task is to tack down the specific problem behaviors ("presenting concerns" in mental health lingo) and to provide some understanding of the condition and its scope to the participants.

The process can be distilled into three questions:

1) What are the specific behaviors the child is showing that are causing him/her repeated difficulty managing the demands of daily life?

In David's case, I'd flesh out what the mother offered over the phone. (Examples of my questions are in italics.) *He talks during group instruction? How often does this occur?* Mom reports that David frequently interrupts the teacher and that the interruptions are out of sync with the control shown by his peers in the same situation. *What are the comments he's making? Are they pertinent to the topic being discussed or is he calling out because he hears something, anything, that he thinks he knows and immediately wants to say something?* The teacher's report was that many times David's remarks are silly and off-topic; it seems as if he's just calling attention to himself *Do you feel that he always needs to be interacting with you in order to stay with something? Are there any activities that he can stay with independently?* If mom's answer to the last question is "Yes, video games," I now have a sense of just how much external structure this child requires in order to engage fully in a life activity.

In Melissa's case, the mother had commented on her daughter not wanting to expend effort to perform the kinds of school work that may have what I describe as "less inherent structure" than other types of academic tasks. (The example mother gave was studying for social studies or science tests.) Given that observation, I'd want to know more about what happens with Melissa's effort on tasks that are discrete and clearly defined. *For example, is it easier for Melissa to start a page of multiplication problems than it is to*

---

2   Both forms of ADHD are included in the Diagnostic and Statistical Manual of Psychiatric Disorders, Fifth Edition. The DSM-5 is the comprehensive handbook of psychiatric disorders which mental health professionals use to make psychiatric diagnoses.

quiz herself about magnets using the teacher's review sheets? Why is this important?
Because if meaningful differences in effort are seen based on the "inherent structure" of the task being performed, then I've gotten valuable information about how life tasks can be modified to help Melissa deploy effort more easily, and I've gotten some information about the severity of her inattentive symptoms.

Regarding behavior at home, I will ask about the specificity and timing of the directions parents have given to get Melissa moving on her morning routine of getting dressed and out to the bus. *Are they reacting to her dawdling with more frequent and exasperated reminders? Or have they experimented with planning out and practicing the tasks she needs to do each morning, so that she become completely familiar with the activity sequences and timing in advance?*

With both Melissa and David, sorting out the specific factors that affect the expression of symptoms begins the process of defining specific interventions to reduce them. Moreover, engaging in the process begins to orient everyone to the idea that dealing with the situation involves the interplay between: 1) the task to be done, 2) the nature of the individual's condition and 3) how parents respond. All three must be considered if meaningful, lasting changes are to occur. Right away, I'm trying to get everyone on board with the notion there is nothing simple or circumscribed about the management of these symptoms because they reflect the presence of a condition more far-reaching in its impact than they may have thought initially when the diagnosis was first made.

Now, on to Question 2:

2) How long have these behaviors been present? Has anything else been going on in the child's life that might contribute to his/her problems at school? Parental discord? Recent hardship? Medical issues in either the child or parent? Death in the family?

Even when preexisting diagnostic evaluations have confirmed the presence of ADHD, I always ask parents and older patients about duration of symptoms. I do this partly to double check (consistent with DSM-5 guidelines) 1) that symptoms of hyperactivity/impulsivity and/or inattention have in fact been recurrently present prior to age twelve and 2) that they affect the child's functioning in at least two situations (e.g., home and school). Assuming that I hear answers consistent with the guidelines, my next question is about other stressors that might be contributing to a child's difficulties.

Given that ADHD is a brain-based delay affecting ones functioning (what is referred to as a neurodevelopmental disorder), the presence of external stressors naturally adds to the burden of managing this condition. I often see this when a family is experiencing stress (e.g., parent's loss of employment or medical disease diagnosis). How a parent responds in this situation can either exacerbate or reduce the stressor's impact on the child.

Paying attention to the bigger picture supports another of my treatment objectives. Early on I try to orient parents and patients to think about ADHD management as varying with circumstances. I encourage them to view their actions and responses to outside stressors as having a crucial role in how the child will handle the demands placed on him/her. For example, maintaining consistent routines for homework and bedtime is always a good idea, but it is particularly important during a parent's radiation treatment for breast cancer. Why? Because to do so shores up and protects a vulnerable, internally distracted child from the toxic effects of becoming even more unmotivated and disengaged due to the impact of the parent's illness. And while it is true that maintaining consistent routines benefits everyone in the family, including siblings without ADHD, the child with ADHD has a narrower bandwidth of resiliency to manage shifts in family life, thus making it all the more important to keep structures in place.

Finally, Question 3:

3) Does anyone else in the family have these kinds of difficulties with impulsivity or inattention? If the child is adopted (as are a high percentage of children in my practice), what do we know about the birth parents regarding issues with behavior or adjustment?

Asking and answering this question helps me get a "read" on factors that can directly affect treatment. Why? Let me explain. First, ADHD is a highly heritable condition as indicated in research studies on first degree family members of children with ADHD and identical twin studies. For example, more than 20 years ago, Joseph Biederman and colleagues found that if one parent has ADHD, there was a 57% chance of offspring having the condition. Since then, research studies have continued to support the finding that genetics play a large role in ADHD.

That said, a parent's awareness of his/her ADHD can vary greatly depending on the severity of the condition, the parent's age and capacity to compensate for difficulties associated with ADHD, and the degree of environmental structure that the parent experienced as a child. In suburban Philadelphia where my office is located, nearly all of the parents in my practice have attended college and many are successful professionals. If their formal education predated the mid-1980's, there's a good chance that problems with procrastination and/or impulsivity were never connected to ADHD. In fact, I have had any number of parents who identified the condition in themselves only after coming to understand it in their child. This is especially true if the parent has superior intellectual ability and was able to navigate formal education reasonably well.

By asking this question early in the treatment process and explaining the high heritability of the condition and how its presentation can vary among family members, I get parents thinking about themselves through the lens of behavior regulation. Even if they are unaware or defensive about acknowledging any past difficulties, opening up the conversation diminishes the "foreign to us" quality that can separate parents from their children emotionally, especially if this diagnosis is new to them all. And as you have already sensed in this chapter, and will see in the chapters on behavior management and family dynamics, I am all about creating a sense of shared mission and team work when confronting the challenges associated with ADHD.

Here's how a physician father in my practice described his dawning awareness of his own mild, nevertheless extant, ADHD. The father's name is Robert and his son's name is Brett.

"As I came to understand the impact that Brett's ADHD was having on his school achievement, I realized I had experienced the same types of problems, albeit in somewhat different ways. My grades in college weren't as strong as they should have been given my ability. In high school, I recall not doing as well on the National Merit Scholarship test as I wanted to, and my score kept me from earning a scholarship. Knowing what I know now about ADHD, I can see that mild ADHD was present, and it held me back academically particularly in high school and college."

Robert attended college with his wife Janet, who also recognized the condition in her husband, recalling his work habits, dorm room and options for medical school.

"Robert was so smart, but relative to me he often had trouble getting himself moving on his course work, leaving studying to the last minute. The floor of his dorm room was covered with old copies of *The New York Times*. When it came time to apply to medical school, I was concerned about where he would get in, or even if he would be admitted to a U.S. medical school. If Robert didn't get into medical school, he would lose his student deferment and would be eligible for the draft. I remember worrying about the possibility of his being sent to Vietnam, saying to myself, 'The rice paddies are calling.'"

I'll end this chapter with a pop quiz. Can you identify some of the core symptoms of ADHD, and can you explain how they can vary among individuals sharing ostensibly the same diagnosis? If you can, pat yourself on the back. You're ready to tackle the next big concept: ADHD as a disorder of behavior regulation.

CHAPTER 2
Essential theory about ADHD:
What you really need to know

ADHD is about behavior regulation

Behavior regulation is my overarching term to describe the core problems that children with attention disorders have "fitting in." How do these kids make their naturally-occurring behavior patterns meet the demands of family, school and peers? And it's not just about behavior; it also involves emotional responses and related actions. Controlling anger or excitement shares similarities with controlling foot tapping or holding back from interrupting someone who is speaking to you. Of course, strong emotions and actions occur together all the time, often requiring inhibitory control in order to bring about an adaptive outcome (e.g., Think of a professional tennis player inhibiting the urge to curse and throw her racquet when she thinks an umpire has made a bad call.)

Where hyperactive-impulsive behaviors are most prominent, the mismatch between behavior patterns and environmental demands falls under a heading I call "too much behavior." Examples include moving about when seated or when a task requires stillness, or talking when listening is appropriate (e.g., David-type behavior).

Alternatively when inattentive behaviors prevail, I refer to the mismatch as "too little initiative, too little sustained effort." Problems here thwart the child's ability to start, continue and complete tasks, thus setting him/her up for negative reactions from others (e.g., Melissa-type behavior). To no one's surprise, research studies with ADHD children suggest that loss of persistence is most evident on tasks that the youngsters found repetitive and boring. What's more, if youngsters with ADHD do not receive immediate consequences (reinforcement) for their persistence, their response rate declines precipitously.

An inability to inhibit lies at the heart of too much behavior, and delays in its development take an ever increasing toll on a child's functioning as he or she ages. For inattentive symptoms, current thinking posits that deficient motivation and weaknesses in working memory play key roles, but other factors (e.g., slow mental processing) are also the subject of current research.

Although experts in the field theorize that the core deficit underlying inattentive and hyperactive-impulsive symptoms differ, I find that they share a common impact – the disruption of purposeful or goal-directed behavior. For that reason, I think it makes sense to construe both forms as originating from some type of constitutionally-based regulatory weakness.

Understanding ADHD as a problem of behavior regulation reduces the risk of "not seeing the forest for the trees", a problem which occurs all too often when too much emphasis is placed on particular symptoms. For example take some of the standard ADHD symptoms: "does not remain seated when necessary;" "interrupts often;" "is easily distracted;" and "does not seem to be listening." To my ears they sound like satellites shooting around a sky of potential behavior patterns. Not only do they seem disconnected from one another, they are dissimilar; any logical person would wonder what they have to do with one another.

My understanding changes, however, when two shifts are made. First, link the symptoms together under the heading of behavior regulation and, second, define behavior regulation in accessible, clear language which clarifies the basis for the linkages. Now I can observe different behaviors (running around versus being forgetful) and see that they share a neurobiological connection.

Understanding ADHD as a behavior regulation disorder also allows patients and parents to get a handle on what I call the "scope" problem of this condition. That is, these difficulties with "too much behavior" and/or "too little initiative and effort" tend to be present throughout the day, even though they may or may not be compromising one's functioning directly depending on what one is doing. This is as true for adults with this condition as it is for children and adolescents.

Not surprisingly, the challenge of behavior regulation rises when activities require greater effort to initiate and sustain. At the very low end of the continuum are highly interactive activities like, video games and social networking. At the other end are tasks requiring a plan and structure: an outline for a business proposal; a two-paragraph condolence letter to a friend whose mother has died; a summary of the key points from a teacher's lesson. For these tasks, an individual needs to generate a plan of action, and then produce, guide and direct the output through to completion If these types of tasks are relatively simple for you, it may be tough to grasp just how difficult they are for individuals with ADHD. However, if you can construe ADHD as a behavior regulation disorder and imagine how significantly it disrupts the internal mental processes that permit controlled verbal expression (such as writing), then the difficulties the person with ADHD faces may begin to make more sense to you.

In psychiatry's handbook of mental disorders (the DSM-5), ADHD is diagnosed in childhood and adolescence as six of nine symptoms in two categories: inattention and hyperactivity/impulsivity.[3] While best practices require endorsement of the DSM-5 criteria in order to confirm a diagnosis, those criteria alone do not capture the breadth of ADHD as a disorder of behavior regulation. The condition is more complex than simply checking a list of symptoms. At the same time however, the symptoms are very useful during the initial process of making a correct diagnosis. And some of the items--such as being unable to remain seated, interrupting others, and appearing not to listen--can be meaningful markers of more encompassing difficulties with behavior regulation.

Finally an exclusive focus on symptoms (e.g., what are they; how often do they occur) can have the unintended but real consequence of trivializing a child's problem, which in turn can limit a caring adult's ability to appreciate the scope of the condition's impact. What do I mean? It sounds like this in my office:

"Well, Dr. Sutherland, his teacher says he falls off his chair during math instruction and tries to get the other kids' attention. When I work with him at home, well yes, he fidgets in his seat and protests having to do homework. But we do get it done. Isn't he just being a little boy?"

The fact that symptoms can vary depending on a child's situation does not, in and of itself, rule out an ADHD diagnosis. Rather, variable symptoms should push parents, teachers and doctors to scrutinize a child's behavior even more closely in order to understand just what is going on. And to that end, having a definition of ADHD as a behavior regulation disorder can assist these key players in evaluating not only a child's overall functioning, but most importantly whether he or she can adjust their behavior to fit with the demands of their world.

No caring adult wants to "pathologize" the variations in a child's everyday behavior. Unfortunately, though, with ADHD it is all too easy to minimize a problem based on situational variability and then miss making a diagnosis at an age when it could spare a child years of academic and social difficulties. I wish the diagnostic process was more straightforward, but the truth is that many times it is not. I always remind myself that children are totally dependent on the adults in their world to make the right call. So we owe it to them and ourselves not to shrink from the challenge.

The core theory of ADHD

In 1997, Russell Barkley took on the herculean task of providing a unified theory of ADHD. In *ADHD and the Nature of Self-Control,* he proposed a model of Attention-Deficit/Hyperactivity Disorder that intertwined concepts of mental abilities and impairments. What made his book transformational in 1997, and why it has maintained its currency, has to do with its breadth. Barkley explains not only ADHD but also the nature of the internal mental processes (referred to as "executive functions") that are responsible for guiding and directing complex behavior--what you and I see as manifestations of self-control. What's more, anything you do that requires coordinating a

---

3   For individuals 17 years of age or older, only 5 symptoms in each category are required.

series of steps over time (making a pot of coffee or writing your first resume) requires the efficient operation of these executive functions in order to get the job done.

In order to provide an overview of his model that was both informative and accessible, I simplified many aspects of his complex formulation (particularly the nature of executive functions). In doing so, I knew I risked potentially "cannibalizing" Dr. Barkley's work. In the end, though, I decided the risk was worth taking because his framework is essential to understanding ADHD as a disorder of behavior regulation.

The diagram below is my attempt to summarize some central aspects of Barkley's model. (The original can be found in Appendix 1.) There are three major components:

> Behavioral inhibition at the top;
> Executive functions (the four boxes in the middle); and
> Motor/Behavioral Control (bottom box).

I realize the language can be a bit arcane, but let's focus on some key concepts that I think are helpful in understanding the disorder.

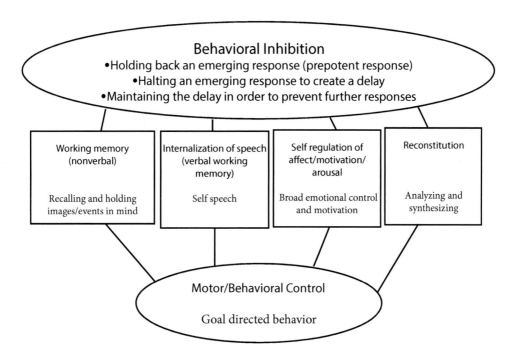

Simplified version of the complete model of executive functions (boxes) and the relationship of these four functions to the behavioral and motor control systems. Adapted from "ADHD and the nature of self-control" by Barkley, R.A., 1997, p. 191. Copyright 1997 Guilford Press. (Reprinted with permission of Guilford Press.)

My adaptation of Barkley's model

Let's start at the top with Behavioral Inhibition, which Barkley considers the primary executive function deficit in ADHD. Behavioral inhibition refers to the capacity to suppress your first impulse to act so that you can think through what you want to do before you do it.

Behavioral inhibition makes possible the second component of Barkley's model: the executive functions,[4] which he defines as internal mental processes in four interacting "domains." Again, in plain language, executive functions are the mental processes we use to guide and shape behaviors.

The four interacting domains are:
1) Nonverbal working memory (holding and manipulating images/events in one's mind)
2) Verbal working memory (holding and manipulating words in one's mind)
3) Emotional regulation (including motivation)
4) Reconstitution, which basically refers to analysis (breaking up ideas into sub-parts) or synthesis (combining sub-part ideas into a larger whole)

Let's spend a few minutes on executive functions; they are critical to understanding the condition and my approach to treatment. (We'll return later to the third component, "Motor/Behavioral Control.")

Executive Functions #1 & #2: Working Memory

Working memory is the ability to hold information in your mind long enough so it can be utilized to accomplish an objective. You use your working memory to accomplish all kinds of goals in life. One everyday example is rehearsing a new phone number in order to enter it into your phone. In baking, it would be reminding yourself about optimal oven temperature and baking time for whatever it is you are making. The point is you have a goal (making a phone call or baking the perfect butterscotch brownie) and working memory (verbal and nonverbal) is a mental workhorse you routinely use to reach your objective. Let's define each kind of working memory more completely.

Non-verbal working memory

To varying degrees, we all can generate mental representations of objects and events. Iconic images (Statue of Liberty or Apple's corporate logo) are easier to conjure up due to repeated exposure. Likewise, seminal events in one's life (a graduation picture or the first time you held your newborn child) often leave lasting visual and sensory impressions.

To give you a new, but immediate, experience of putting your non-verbal memory to work, let's try the following exercise. Close your eyes and see if you can formulate a

---

4   In 2012, Barkley added self awareness as an executive function and now combines it with the other four executive functions. Barkley's original model can be found in Appendix 1.

mental image of the White House--the triangular shape on the front, the two wings on either side of the building, and the semi-circular driveway where heads of state exit their limos to enter the building.

Now conjure that same image of the White House, but place it in the midst of a swirling snowstorm.

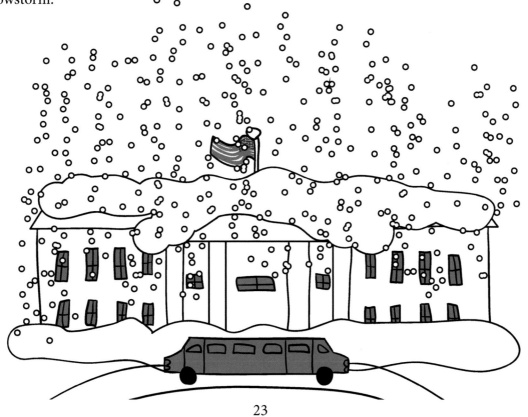

Now, subtract the snowstorm and imagine that the West side of the residence has been painted periwinkle blue while the East side is peony pink.

With this example, your ultimate goal might be a creative product. Let's say you are an author/illustrator writing a children's book about an invisible boy with supernatural powers living undetected with the First Family. Manipulating imagery of the White House in your head might help you develop aspects of the book's plot or provide images you want to sketch. Or alternatively, maybe your goal is short-term and doing this provides a diversion while you are sitting in an airport waiting for a delayed flight. An important point here, is that the ability to initiate, sustain and engage in these mental activities frees an individual from being at the mercy of responding immediately to events in the outside world.

Verbal working memory

Language is also available to help guide and shape our behavior. As such, images held in the mind can also be supported with words.

To illustrate this, let's move away from generating images of the White House to a different example, something each of us does, nearly every day: the "To Do" list. Imagine making a "To Do" list of errands for a Saturday morning: deposit check and get cash at ATM, drop off a sweater at

24

the dry cleaner, pick up repaired earrings at the jeweler, buy the good balsamic vinegar for the roasted beet salad you are making for dinner. In addition to whatever images you might form in your mind about the errands, words also support your activity. Say you leave your "To Do" list in the car while shopping, and are about to leave without the balsamic vinegar. Talking to yourself in your head, you ask, "What else was on that list? Earrings, check. Sweater, check…Balsamic vinegar, ??" And off you go to the gourmet store for the vinegar.

In short, that's what verbal working memory can provide: words either spoken or in thought that remind and therefore guide and shape actions.

Executive Function #3: Emotional Regulation

The third domain in Barkley's concept of executive functions is emotional regulation. In this context, emotional regulation refers to the ways in which we use our emotions in service of a goal. Individuals with ADHD often have difficulty managing their emotions, particularly the negative ones such as anger, sadness, guilt and shame. Anxiety is also an emotion that can be exacerbated by ADHD, particularly if the individual already possesses it as a co-morbid condition.

As I see it, one of the major factors affecting emotional regulation has to do with behavioral inhibition: how readily can a person halt and impose a delay in responding when that individual is experiencing an intense emotional response to say, anger or fear. I will give you an example from my own life. It's a beautiful summer day at the New Jersey shore, and I have just finished a walk down a lovely stretch of beach and return to my parked bicycle. I put my backpack containing a little money and my mobile phone in my bike basket. My legs are getting itchy from the sand, so once home, I jump off the bike, rush to the hose and spray my legs.

I was also quite hungry at this point, so I leave my backpack outside on a small table near the house. Once showered and fed, I start to think about my phone and the backpack. As I look around and fail to find it, fear and dread build quickly and I rush to the bike and see the basket is empty. I start to panic, jump in the car and rush back to the beach entrance where I had parked my bike earlier.

No backpack. "Thieves," I seethe under my breath, recalling a time when my small sailboat had been stolen off a bay beach. I was hurtling toward more and more unregulated, unhelpful negative emotion, when I decided to pull the car over and take what I call in my practice a "STOP." As with Barkley's model, I halted all of the catastrophic thinking going on in my head and insisted with myself that I maintain a state with key emotions in check. I then reviewed what I had done when I got home – the hose, the table, the backpack! I drove home and there it was.

Remember that I said the executive functions interact with one another. In my example, it's plain to see that if I did not halt the outpouring of panic and distress, my working memory (both images and words) could not have operated effectively to help me reach the goal of locating my backpack.

Most of you probably can recall a similar experience, but have you ever really thought about the vital importance of the braking and delaying mechanism of behavior inhibition in conjunction with the management of emotions and problem-solving? Individuals with ADHD experience emotions such as anger, frustration and impatience before they can summon the internal mental processes needed to slow down and reevaluate how to respond, usually in a way that leads to better outcomes.

Another core aspect of emotional regulation involves motivation, the summoning up of effort and sustained engagement with a task. Those individuals with predominantly inattentive forms of ADHD struggle mightily with this aspect, suffering repeated blows to their self-confidence as episode after episode of not accomplishing tasks pile up. Unlike halting an intense negative emotion (e.g., panic that you may have lost your phone), breaking a pattern of low motivation requires a different type of stop mechanism. For folks with high levels of inattentive symptoms, whatever catches their eye is where they go. Intention to do effortful tasks evaporates if something more interesting comes along. What has to be halted is the predilection to shift and drift. And the individual has to name and actively devise, in advance, workarounds and rewards to keep the tendency to shift and drift in check.

Executive Function #4: Reconstitution

Barkley's fourth domain of executive function is reconstitution, which he has recently defined as... "a process of initially taking apart (analysis) then recombining information (synthesis) to form novel and potentially useful recombinations." (Barkley, 2015, pp. 415-416) [5] "Analysis" can be thought of as breaking down the components of a multi-step task and identifying each one. A simple example I like to use is to magine the sequence of steps in making a pot of coffee. My process goes like this: fill the coffee maker with water; insert a paper filter in its holder; measure ground coffee into the filter; close the top and flip the switch to "on." Analyze the steps in your mind and then read them off, turning each step into an action that supports the ultimate goal of making a pot of coffee. This process of analyzing tasks by breaking them down into sequential, component steps is the foundation for executing familiar, multi-step tasks. We humans use it constantly.

But let's say I wanted to mix it up and buy whole beans and grind the coffee at home. Now the internal mental activity of synthesis or adding/replacing steps in a process comes into play, since this process needs to be altered to include the bean grinding step. The "mental play" of breaking down component steps and adding, subtracting or substituting other steps set the conditions for goal attainment and creative problem solving. As with the other executive functions, however, full access to this process rests on the capacity to halt and delay one's immediate reactions in life.

Goal-directed Behavior

All of the internal mental processes we have just reviewed govern our outward behavior. So let's return to the bottom section of Barkley's model, labeled "Motor/Behavioral Control." This is my simplification of Barkley's parlance for goal-directed behavior. The operation of two complex mental abilities control observable goal-directed behavior: the

---

5   Barkley, R.A. (2015) Executive functioning and self-regulation viewed as an extended phenotype: Implications of the theory for ADHD and its treatment, in Barkley, R.A. (Ed.) *Attention-deficit hyperactivity disorder: A handbook for diagnosis and treatment* (4th ed.). New York: Guilford Press.

ability to inhibit an immediate response while also performing executive functions which shape behavior. Any controlled output--from changing how you make a pot of coffee to creating an outline for a paper to figuring out how you will get X number of chores done in Y number of minutes--requires some measure of maintaining inhibition of action, related or unrelated to the task, while other processes operate to guide and direct the behavior toward the results we seek.

Goal-directed behaviors that are age appropriate will include a capacity for flexibility in problem solving, an ability to ignore irrelevant, potentially disruptive responses, and an ability to fit others' feedback into one's goal-directed activity. In contrast, without the smooth development of behavioral inhibition, growth of the executive functions will be hampered, impairing goal-directed behavior. If inhibitory control remains weak during a child's development, he or she is at risk of losing ground relative to peers because their executive functions are not developing in age-expected ways.

And that's exactly what ADHD confers. It results in impairment of the most basic capacity to inhibit immediate responses. This inability to inhibit responses, in turn, gives rise to a developmental lag in the growth of both forms of working memory and in the capacity to regulate one's emotions and motivation, as well as in the thinking processes that allow us to analyze and synthesize new responses.

Behavioral regulation, executive functions and ADHD

In the late 1990's with Barkley's model as my guide, the relationship between behavioral inhibition and executive functions began to take center stage in my understanding and treatment of ADHD. Now, as then, my views about ADHD as a disorder of behavior regulation follow directly from Barkley's thinking about the role that executive functions play.

Specifically, he states:

"These executive functions provide for human 'self-regulation' defined as (1) any action one directs at oneself (2) in order to change subsequent behavior (3) so as to alter a distant or delayed consequence and thereby maximize those consequences." (Barkley, 2015, p.87)[6]

At first read, Barkley's reference to "any action one directs at oneself" is a puzzle. What does he mean by that phrase? The answer can be found in the first part of the sentence: "These executive functions provide for human self-regulation." "Actions directed to oneself" often are thinking processes that can be used to guide and shape behavior that has yet to occur. Why do we do this? We do this in order to bring about a result that is usually more desirable and efficacious than if we just act in the moment on an immediate response.

---

6   Barkley, R.A. (2015) Emotional dysregulation is a core component of ADHD. In Barkley, R.A. (Ed.) (2015) *Attention-deficit hyperactivity disorder: A handbook for diagnosis and treatment (4th ed.)*. New York: Guilford Press.

For as much as Barkley's model influenced my thinking, I also reviewed the work of other neuroscientists. I was drawn to the work of Adele Diamond, a prominent Canadian neuropsychologist who through her long professional career has emphasized the impact of biological and environmental factors on executive functions. She became another of my "go to" thinkers on the topic. Diamond describes three core executive functions: inhibitory control (or simply inhibition), working memory and cognitive flexibility.

Inhibitory control pertains to the ability to shut down the impulse to act in response to compelling external stimuli. Working memory refers to holding information in mind in order to manipulate it mentally. (That both of these core executive functions overlap with Barkley's definitions and thinking was conceptually satisfying.) Moreover, Diamond noted that the development of inhibitory control and working memory occur before the emergence of the third core executive function, cognitive flexibility. Indeed, inhibitory control and working memory are the foundation for building cognitive flexibility, which refers to one's capacity to shift point of view by holding back what is unfolding as a dominant thought in order to take account of other information and hold it in mind.

To illustrate Diamond's executive functions, here's an example from everyday life. Let's say you are trying to add regular exercise to your daily routine, but feel you can't find the time to do it.

To solve this problem, you need to hold back the dominant thought (no time to exercise), review your daily schedule with an eye towards looking for even a small window of open time, and then figure out what exercise (running outside or rowing on a machine) could fit into that block of time.

For Diamond, the triad of core executive functions lays the ground work for the development of higher order executive functions such as reasoning, planning and problem solving. (Barkley makes similar arguments about developmental hierarchies in the growth of executive functions.) This idea of core executive functions laying the groundwork for the development of more sophisticated ones--well, that set off a firestorm inside my brain as it related to treatment. Specifically, delays in the growth of executive functions stack up on themselves. If you don't develop inhibitory control, then your cognitive flexibility will be curtailed, which then means that higher-order planning and problem-solving will be adversely affected. Oh lord, I thought, so many bases to cover as the child potentially loses more ground with advancing age.

Along with expanding my understanding of executive functions, another issue gnawed at me. Are weaknesses in executive function always indicative of ADHD? Currently neuroscientists are wrestling with this question. In my reading of the research, combined with many hours of clinical work, I believe there may be occasional cases (such as a diagnosis of recurrent bouts of depression) where executive function weaknesses do not follow from an ADHD diagnosis. But in the overwhelming majority of cases in my practice, they do and the evidence is there from the moment I start taking a history and am told presenting concerns. Real-time weaknesses with task initiation, task completion, and impulsive actions that disrupt goals are mentioned first, and usually their impact is neither mild nor circumscribed. My case notes overflow with these examples and they repeat themselves.

To put it mildly, it is difficult to explain this information to families. My struggle to describe the relationship between ADHD, broad delays in neurodevelopment and disruption in growth of executive functions led me to create the following chart. Some may not agree completely with this "reduction" in the complexity, but at least for my families with adolescents, it seems to provide a toehold in terms of understanding these relationships.

ADHD and its Relationship to Executive Functions

1) Disorder is ADHD--a condition leading to pervasive problems with behavior and emotional regulation, most notably being held hostage to real-time reactions to life's demands. Outward manifestations of it can seem paradoxical--either showing in some cases "too much behavior" or "too little initiative/too little sustained effort." At times one or the other is more prominent. ADHD is underpinned by...

2) ...Delays in the development of fundamental capacities that allow us to stop and start our behavioral and emotional patterns. Behavioral inhibition is a key master executive function affecting this form of neurodevelopment. The neurodevelopmental capacities allow one to build other executive functions, and when delays occur, they give rise to...

3) ...Impairments in growth of executive functions, which in turn disrupts goal-direct-ed output. Over time, delays in the growth of neurodevelopmental capacities give rise to impairments in the growth of executive functions (the internal mental processes which allow us to guide and direct our behavior).

As we move deeper into the 21st century, Russell Barkley, Adele Diamond and other researchers will continue to refine their concepts about behavioral inhibition and executive functions: what they are; why they developed; how they develop and how they relate to one another. Given this current state of affairs, I continue to think that adopting a broad definition of ADHD (disorder of behavior regulation) is helpful because it provides room for modifications to our understanding of the condition and its internal mental processes (executive functions). At the same time, it is sufficiently practical and all-encompassing to describe the overt symptoms that are manifested in everyday life.

Other Considerations:
Development, environmental structure and task variability and severity

With the core theory in hand, we are now in a position to look at other factors that affect humans' ability to guide and direct our behavior. Development, environmental structure, and task variability and severity are three major factors in regulating behavior. Let's examine the impact of each on the expression of ADHD in real world-type settings.

Development

One of the singular joys of parenthood is watching your child grow and develop. First words turn into phrases; standing turns into toddling and thinking skills blossom as little ones discover their world. I distinctly remember when my 2-year-old son brought home his first painting from day care, "an abstract" comprised of orange and red circles. I was over the moon about the idea that he could now "represent" a geometric shape with a paint brush. Likewise, when I got a report from my daughter's preschool teacher that she remembered all the words and carried the tunes to the holiday songs the class was singing, I beamed with pride at the advance in memory development that this denoted.

That said, individual differences in development can also cause consternation, as when a 3-year-old's ability to hit pitched softballs exceeds his ability to put together puzzles or string words together in sentences. Fortunately for parents, pediatricians (bless them) provide periodic reality checks on how advanced, average or delayed a child's development appears across various domains. For large many children, delays are often transient. Concerns parents raise about their two year old can evaporate by age five. In fact, if parents haven't kept a record of what happened and when, they often don't recall much about a relatively short-lived delay. I see this all the time as part of the developmental histories I receive from parents during intake sessions.

Growth in behavior regulation, just as in other domains (e.g., speech, gross motor and fine motor), develops in ways that psychologists and neuroscientists have been tracking with ever greater levels of specificity. Unlike other areas, however, sorting out a typical trajectory is complicated by the nature of what we are observing: behavior regulation. As we have seen, these are processes that guide and direct speech, imagery, emotional control and thinking skills, which means they can be tough to measure, particularly in a way that is meaningful for functioning in daily life.

For example, how do you measure age-appropriate behavior for a child not interrupting their mother when she is on the phone? Under normal circumstances many parents might say that no interruptions would be the standard for a short call (with no emergencies) for a child age 7 or 8. How do we know this? Developmental timetables such as that offered by psychologists, Peg Dawson and Richard Guare, in their book on executive functions indicate that in the period between kindergarten and grade 2, children become capable of accomplishing "inhibit behaviors" such as following safety rules, holding back from swearing, and raising a hand before speaking in class. By that standard, holding back from speaking when a parent is on the phone should be well within the average second grader's grasp, assuming no emergencies and a reasonable, rather than lengthy, call duration. But start lowering the age by increments of 1-2 years, and it becomes difficult to say what standard is consistently reasonable for a younger 6 or older 5 year-old. That said, most of us can imagine that such a standard is too high for a 3 or 4 year-old, and for a 2-year-old--well forget about it. Engaging in this exercise, however, demonstrates just how difficult it is for parents to gauge clearly what is age-appropriate behavior regulation. Add to this the fact that the amount of environmental structure present in any situation can have a significant impact on a child's regulatory ability, and the developmental issue becomes even more complicated.

Environmental Structure

What do I mean by "environmental structure?" In the previous phone call example, I'm referring to items such as the following: 1) How much advance notice was given to the child about the upcoming call? 2) Was the child informed about the "no-interruption" expectation and did they show awareness that they had absorbed it? 3) And was the child engaged in another activity of high interest during the call that might have helped prevent the possibility of interruption?

Parents know where I'm going here--they reflexively do the kinds of things I'm suggesting by the above questions when they need periods without interruption at home for their own personal or vocational needs. But evaluating a child's ability to execute this expected behavior starts to become a concern when, time after time and at an age where following a no-interruption request seems reasonable, the child either doesn't comply at all or can't sustain compliance for a short period of time. Comments such as "he (or she) is immature" make their way into a parent's remarks about their child, as does worry about the impact this will have on their functioning socially and academically down the road. It remains a murky business for a parent to sort out when a lag in growth constitutes a true red flag or just a lapse in providing enough environmental structure.

Task variability and severity of symptoms

Thinking about the impact of environmental structure brings up another critical variable affecting behavior regulation: variable performance on tasks depending whether they are relatively easy or hard to initiate. This issue goes back to the video game conundrum I discussed earlier. Why can a child inhibit and sustain interest while playing video games but not when practicing math facts even when there is a big test the next day? As noted, part of this attention difference derives from the nature of ADHD, a condition that makes it much easier to engage in highly interactive activities with proximate rewards.

Given this, parents of children with ADHD will help themselves enormously if they either avoid or modify low-structure, boring situations (e.g., sitting through a concert or a sermon in church) that are sure to tax their child's regulatory capacity. While some situations, such as a close relative's wedding ceremony cannot be avoided, parents can avert trouble by figuring out workarounds. Examples of workarounds include limiting how much participation is required of the child in the event, or allowing them to engage in activities without disturbing others. Obviously over time the child will need to learn how to manage "boring" activities and to participate in events they don't find interesting.

However, that doesn't preclude a parent from making smart choices about situations they know from experience will be tough for their child to manage.

Finally, the severity of the ADHD itself, which varies from mild to severe, will affect how easily each child can initiate low preference activities. Children with severe levels of ADHD demonstrate nearly constant, significant difficulty regulating themselves across many situations in life. Their problems are manifest everywhere: yelling for help to get dressed in the morning; frequently forgetting lunchboxes; standing up when asked to stay seated on the bus; calling out in

33

class; not finishing their seat work; resisting the initiation of homework; and complaining/dawdling while getting ready for bed. All day long you see it.

And in a way, the "moderate-to-severe" kids are the lucky ones for exactly that reason. Their regulation problems are evident all day long, and they cause ongoing agitation to the child, his peers and the adults in charge of him. Not so, however, for those youngsters with mild forms of ADHD, especially if the presentation is of the inattentive variety. Unless and until the too-little-initiative, too-little-effort they are showing begins to have a recurrent, major impact on their functioning (usually in the form of declining academic achievement), these children move through their lives--sometimes missing wide swaths of what is going on around them or, losing confidence--but largely unaware of problems with behavior regulation. (Examples of these difficulties may be found in Chapter 5 from Amy and Beth. Skip ahead and read them now if you are interested.)

Other considerations -- "One young woman's tale"

Finally, the aforementioned factors interact with one another and are evident in the histories and comments made in my office. While in high school, Susan, a 22 year old with ADHD (Predominantly inattentive presentation), experienced milder symptoms, an absence of frank learning problems and a superior range verbal and general intellectual ability. Although she entered a prestigious university with AP credits, she confronted surprising "transition" problems that were far greater than she or her parents ever would have thought possible. Listen to what Susan has to say about her experience moving from high school to college:

"A good example of what seems like a relatively contained 'satellite symptom' is the ADHD tendency which Dr. Sutherland calls 'shift and drift.' If you've done well in school previously, you just don't realize how big a problem it is; how it is clearly a major aspect of your overall behavior regulation. For example, in a film studies class in college, I tried to start an outline of points to be covered for my paper on visibility and the movie *Scream*. But instead of sticking to my goal of getting my major points on paper, I got lost watching Netflix. Though I knew I wasn't accomplishing the goal, the more I drifted, the more I just got lost in doing the 'off-task' stuff.

And you might think, well so what, all college kids can get distracted by Netflix. But for me, the pattern of shift and drift grew as I became more demoralized about not getting work done. For example, I fell into a pattern of binge watching episodes of *Breaking Bad* to the point that I didn't leave my bed to turn on lights, didn't really eat and stopped going to class.

What I see now is that the whole phenomenon is aggravated when you are experiencing distant-in-time, low reward value for what you are doing. One of the reasons I did much better in high school is because there were so many more evaluations (daily homework, weekly tests) to keep me on track. In college, especially in courses with only a mid-term, final and maybe a paper or two, I couldn't summon the level of motivation needed to accomplish these tasks.

If moderate-to-severe ADHD had been diagnosed with me even as late as middle school or high school, I would've been stressed out and forced to develop compensations, or I would have failed. All this gets compounded when shame is attached to trying to accomplish current goals and you've had goals you couldn't find the motivation to accomplish in the past. With that history, taking on new goals just seems that much more daunting. Pretty soon every failure starts to add up and conspires to bring you down. It's very tough trying to find the optimism and motivation to combat aspects of yourself that you know are laying you low day after day."

As Susan transitioned to university, she did not initially possess the self-awareness to understand that what had seemed to be relatively circumscribed motivational difficulties earlier were actually harbingers of larger, more pervasive problems she would encounter in higher education, where the external structure was greatly reduced relative to high school. Together in treatment, we recognized that she was having trouble grappling with the scope problem of her ADHD, and that in order to overcome her challenges, she would have to take steps to manage her weaknesses actively throughout the day.

CHAPTER 3
ADHD and Behavior Change:
Much more complicated than you might think.

Sensing potential problems but what exactly do you do about it?

Imagine this scene. It's a warm, early summer day, sparkling clear with low humidity. Yesterday was the last day of school and a mother, Sarah, and her 7 year old son M.J. are going to their swim club in the mid-afternoon for some exercise and fellowship. M.J. is an energetic guy who is comfortable with all things "pool." He has already passed his tag test by swimming two lengths in the deep end without stopping and has been doing cannonballs off the diving board for two summers running. He loves the pool and hopes that some rising second grade buddies will be at the club. Goggles, towels, sunscreen, snacks, juice boxes are all packed and off they go for what should be the most pleasant of outings for mother and son.

Lurking at the edges of Sarah's consciousness is the report card that has been sitting on her desk since yesterday. During the spring of this year, M.J.'s first grade teacher had alerted Sarah and her husband Dan that their son was having trouble settling down and completing his seat work in a reasonable amount of time. He was calling out answers or making silly comments during group instruction or morning circle time, and he was constantly getting up to sharpen his pencil even when it didn't need to be sharpened. Dan recalled that he had been like M.J. but Dan, unlike M.J., went to a Catholic school where the teachers were very strict and the day was very structured. Dan remembers "Needs Improvement" comments on his report cards for items such as "Respects the rights of others' or "Displays consistent effort on assignments," but he had gotten by. He was intelligent, did reasonably well academically in high school and college and was a valued player on his lacrosse team in high school and during the first part of college.

All of the preceding information moves in and out of Sarah's mind as she has been getting ready to go to the pool with M.J. Lately, she has been struggling with her own reactions to what is happening to M.J. In the past, she would have short-lived bouts of worry about how her son would fare in any new situation where he must follow rules. But given the end of his school year, the teacher's comments and his report card, Sarah's anxiety is becoming more

of her "constant companion." Moreover, the anxiety is affecting how she feels about M.J. She sees herself doing too much for him and constantly monitoring him. For example, she just went to get the towel he forgot after he was reminded twice to get it. She also sees herself getting angry with him when he's too loud or says something that makes other kids uncomfortable -- he jokingly called a little girl in his class "four eyes" after she started wearing glasses. The girl's mother was not pleased and neither was his teacher.

Back to the outing at hand, Sarah and M.J. are in the car on their way to the pool and Sarah remembers M.J.'s dentist appointment at 4 p.m. She had meant to tell him about it sooner, but she got distracted when she had to run back in to get the forgotten towel. From the front seat then, Sarah mentions to M.J. that they will need to leave the pool by 4 pm because he has a routine dentist appointment at 5 pm. Sarah tacks the time down even more, noting that when the small hand of the pool clock is pointing to the 4 and the big hand is on the 12, that's when they will leave. He makes eye contact with her in the rearview mirror and says, "Yeah," but he is totally focused on the diving board and the new basketball hoop that the club has installed in the shallow end of the pool. He has been talking non-stop about it all the way there.

Once at the pool, M.J.'s physical energy, single-mindedness, and difficulty taking turns (e.g., giving up the ball when his turn is over) are evident throughout the afternoon. Following posted rules also proves challenging. After the first verbal warning, the lifeguard twice has to ask M.J. to sit down since he had been unsafe running on the pool deck.

The swim club has a large clock on the wall facing the aquatic basketball court, and M.J. notices the little hand inching towards the "4" on one of his trips to the diving board, but his mom's comment about the dentist appointment never really registered. Meanwhile, Sarah has met a fellow rising second grade mother and the two are absorbed in a discussion about the change in second grade teaching staff. At 3:50 p.m., mom disengages from her chat and asks MJ to get out of the pool. M.J. launches into a spate of whining and protest which sets his mother's teeth on edge. She reminds M.J. that she told him about the dental appointment in route to the pool and points towards the clock. M.J. starts yelling that he hasn't had enough time swimming and going to the dentist is "dumb." Increasing mother-son conflict ensues with mother pulling M.J. out of the pool and taking him dripping wet but firmly by the hand to the car where M.J. will have to change his clothes. Sarah is exasperated and embarrassed, recalling the number of times she and M.J. have had problems like this in the past.

What's going on here? Why couldn't M.J. bring his behavior in line with his mom's expectations? She had told him about the appointment in the car and he had made eye contact with her when she said it. Why is his reaction so extreme? He has been at the pool for several hours. What's going on inside his head? While it's impossible to say for certain, one element at play is M.J.'s inability to understand time and to cope with the intersection between immediate wants and the upcoming demands of daily living. When these kinds of problems managing transitions recur regularly, then you have at least a "yellow" flag that something is amiss with your child's behavior regulation, well in advance of a formal diagnosis of ADHD.

Understanding and managing time: SOS/danger ahead

But why would this be the case? Why would recurrent difficulties managing transitions carry such weight in terms of suggesting the possible presence of ADHD? The answer comes from neuroscience. Theory and research have shown us that the presence of ADHD disrupts the growth in one's ability both to estimate and monitor the passage of time but also, crucially, to suspend and modify one's immediate responses in order to meet a goal--abilities which depend on the effective operation of executive functions, described in Chapter 2. Okay fine, you might say, but how does a mother like Sarah deal with this issue practically, in the moment? Are there ways to help M.J. compensate for this weakness? The answer is "yes," but first let's deal with a conclusion drawn all too often by individuals watching a child manifesting problems with behavior regulation; namely that M.J.'s difficulties are due to lax discipline on the part of his parents.

Indeed, casual observers of the M.J. "pool exit episode" might be inclined to conclude that M.J. is "spoiled;" i.e., if only his parents were more strict about rules, he wouldn't behave this way. No doubt, a more judgmental observer might assume that there is lax discipline about many things, such as what M.J. eats (e.g., too much junk food), when he goes to bed and how well he takes care of his possessions. While M.J. may not be the easiest kid to manage, what parents know all too well when their kids misbehave is this: their management is implicated in a mental checklist of reasons running through the observer's head as to why this child is acting this way.

Even though parents may know that discipline alone is not the sole issue affecting this child, the inferences of parental mismanagement really sting in the moment, leading to shame and embarrassment. Moreover, repeat experiences of these negative emotions only serve to make a parent like Sarah more dispirited about her relationship with her child, rendering her less able to cope well with him in subsequent stressful interactions.

Given the challenges associated with ADHD and behavior regulation combined with an understandable wish to avoid embarrassment for both child and parents, what steps could parents take to avert or minimize the potential for trouble? Read on – I have a suggestion.

Adopting an "antecedent mindset": Getting specific about planning ahead

While the Sarah/M.J. scenario and background is fictional, I see the elements constantly in the presenting concerns, case histories and therapeutic sessions of the families I treat. I know the sense of dread and discomfort that parents feel when they sense that their child's behavior is not what it should be.

If this is happening to you and you are feeling helpless about what to do, there is one adjustment you can make right away which may help your child regulate his behavior a bit better and allow you to experience a sense of greater control. It is what I call "adopting an antecedent mindset."[7] It simply refers to anticipating known challenges with a plan. More specifically, it means incorporating a way of thinking about your child's behavior which gets out in front of potential challenges in order to avert problems.

All children, by virtue of their developmental status, tend to live more in the here and now. (The developmental psychologist Jean Piaget referred to middle childhood as the concrete operational period where, among other things, cognitive abilities are constrained limiting the child's capacity to reason about non-present or hypothetical events.) But adults--that's a different story. Adults can apply reasoning to past and future events, both those which have occurred, might occur, or those that are the stuff of pure imagination.

Given their enhanced ability to think about non-present events, parents have a big edge cognitively over anyone in the 5-11 year-old set. Specifically, you as the parent can adopt a pervasive habit of anticipating behavior regulation challenges and "managing" them with your child before the events transpire. To flesh this concept out more, let's go back to the Sarah/M.J. scenario. What would Sarah have done differently had she been operating with an antecedent mindset?

First, Sarah would have considered M.J.'s history with compliance to inform the present situation. Assuming that M.J. has had trouble leaving high preference activities (such as the pool) in the past, Sarah would have entered that into her thinking as she was planning the event. (Remember she knew about the dental appointment but got distracted by his towel and forgot to tell M.J. about it, only to recall it when she was driving away.) But backing it up even more, with an antecedent mindset, Sarah would be weighing the pros and cons of even going to the pool in the afternoon prior to a dental appointment. She would be using her adult cognitive ability to imagine just how reasonable the time frame for swimming is given the time needed to change, get dry and get to the dentist.

---

7   As found in The Random House Dictionary, the verb antecede combines two Latin terms, ante and cede to form anteced(ere). It means "to go before in time, order, etc." Antecedent is the adjective form.

Specifically, she would say to herself: How well has M.J. handled these types of situations in the past? She recalls a week ago when M.J. had to get to a soccer practice after his friend Sam's birthday party, and it took him more than an hour to make the transition.

Second, Sarah would prepare M.J. for the afternoon's activities. Children with lags in behavior regulation must be actively encouraged to use words, images, thinking skills and their emotions to help them manage life activities. That said, parents must remember their capacity to do so is limited not only by general development but also the lag in behavior regulation. So Sarah can help M.J. bridge these gaps by sitting him down in a quiet location well in advance of the outing and engaging him in a conversation such as the following.

Sarah establishes good eye contact with M.J. and says, "Would you like to go to the pool this afternoon?"
M.J.: Oh yeah, Mom. Let's go!
Sarah: Okay, I thought you would. But you have a dentist appointment at 4 p.m. today. Last week we had trouble getting to soccer practice after Sam's party. Do you remember what happened?
M.J.: Sort of.
Sarah: What happened?
M.J.: I don't really know; I can't remember.
Sarah: Well, you kept playing basketball when it was time to leave and I had to...do you remember?
M.J.: Yeah. I yelled at you and you got mad.
Sarah: Yes, and then what about getting changed for soccer? Did you get your shorts, jersey, socks and cleats on right away when we got home?
M.J.: I can't remember, but I remember it was bad.
Sarah: Well, no, you didn't get changed quickly. And then what happened? Can you remember?
M.J.: We were late to practice.
Sarah: What did the coach's look like when we were late?
M.J.: Kind of frowning.

Sarah: Okay, so if I'm going to take you to the pool and we have to get to the dentist later in the afternoon, what will you need to do the first time I ask you to get out of the pool?
M.J.: Get out when you ask me.

Sarah: And what about drying off in the locker room and getting clothes on? How will you do that? Slowly and complaining?

M.J. (laughing): No, I put my clothes on quick and tell you I'm ready.

Sarah: Okay, do we have a deal, my buddy?

Sarah: Repeat back to me what you must do when I say time to get out of the pool. I'll help you. First you must…

M.J.: Get out right away.

Sarah: And second you…

M.J.: Go with you to the locker room to dry off.

Sarah: Then you…

M.J.: Pull on my clothes quickly and tell you I'm ready.

Obviously there is no guarantee that the application of an antecedent mindset will always work to avert transition problems. The target of the intervention is two-fold: 1) to help the child compensate (e.g., use words, images, emotions, thinking skills) for weak executive control and 2) to help the parent accommodate to the child's lags in behavior regulation.

Interventions for adults

Compared with children, adults and older adolescents have distinct advantages when it comes to modifying their behavior. Most notably, adults and older adolescents can think about non-present events with greater specificity and accuracy than is possible for their younger counterparts. Referencing Jean Piaget again, he observed the emergence of this capacity (referred to as "formal operations") and understood that its emergence allowed one to think hypothetically. Simple forms of hypothetical reasoning are if-then type statements. Consider this example: an adult hears an evening weather forecast predicting heavy rain late the next day. Even though the sun is shining in the morning, the adult says to themself, "Since heavy rain is predicted later, I will take a raincoat and umbrella to work this morning to be ready for rain on my way home later."

The adult's capacity not only to reason in a particularized way about not-yet-present events, but also to create realistic action steps, allows them to shape a beneficial outcome in the future. While most children can take direction about future events ("Mom says, "Wear my raincoat."), reasoning specifically and developing truly "doable" action steps about what has not yet occurred is more of a stretch for the younger set.

As you read the preceding example, did it trigger thoughts about executive functions (e.g., working memory, analysis and synthesis)? If so, congratulate yourself. If in addition to executive functions, the example got you thinking about weaknesses in those functions and problems in living associated with ADHD, even better. Congratulate yourself again. Making such linkages indicates that you are coming to understand the encompassing nature of regulatory problems faced by adults and older adolescents with ADHD.

But at this point you may be saying to yourself, "Wait a minute. Wasn't this chapter supposed to be about behavior change?" How does making connections between weaknesses in executive functions and ADHD lead to developing interventions for adults? Trust me; it does. Read on.

Getting specific about planning ahead: Here we go again

Recall my concept of an antecedent mindset as applied to the swimming pool episode with M.J. and Sarah, and recall that I suggested that Sarah "specify" with M.J. all the steps to leaving the pool well BEFORE the time to leave. One could say that Sarah was generating words, images and thinking about a set of non-present, but familiar, events. By doing this, Sarah was helping M.J. to access mentally the "leaving-the-pool procedures," a situation which would be recurring soon. But why did Sarah need to take the lead recalling and then re-shaping the steps for M.J.? Because as a rising second grader, M.J. is limited in his ability to think prospectively about non-present events and what he might do, particularly in his ability to change his behavior in the future.

Switch gears now to an adult or an older adolescent, one with diagnosed ADHD who recognizes that their ability to formulate specific plans-of-action is weak. But thanks to the cognitive advances conferred by development, the adult (unlike M.J.) is able to conjure specific words and images to represent future events. (e.g., "I have a dentist appointment next Monday at 8 am.) And that adult can also generate his or her own words and images about what could happen if they fail to write the appointment down in a planner or forget to set a reminder on their phone. (e.g., "I will miss the appointment, be embarrassed, and have to pay a no-show fee.") Notice that I included "be embarassed" in the list of possible outcomes associated with forgetting. Including "embarrassment" is important because management of emotions, an aspect of emotion regulation, needs to be factored into the executive function mix. Indeed, imagining the uncomfortable emotions that could follow from an episode of forgetting might help motivate the adult to take steps in advance which would prevent "forgetting" in the first place.

To summarize then, one modest but nonetheless meaningful intervention for adults with ADHD is a conceptual one involving a major shift in outlook. Going forward in life, adults with ADHD need to take full advantage of their abilities to think hypothetically in order to avert problems and improve outcomes for themselves. Holding fast to this insight and taking steps daily to use it to shape behavior sets the stage for learning how to compensate for the executive function weaknesses. With that in mind, adults are well positioned to begin formulating specific strategies to address the particular challenges they face on a recurrent basis.

Your adult brain with ADHD: Seize the day vs too little too late

Now let's take the adult's new-found appreciation for hypothetical reasoning and combine it with my notions about adopting an antecedent mindset to guide and direct future behavior. (Quick definition: adopting an antecedent mindset is the process of getting out in front of yet-to-occur events by developing potential action steps using words, images, constructive motivation/emotions and thinking.) What advantages does this combination provide, and how does it lead you to modify your behavior?

In terms of advantages, a commitment to using/valuing hypothetical thinking in tandem with the adoption of an antecedent mindset means that you can start to say goodbye to what I call "chasing your symptoms" of ADHD. What do I mean? Well, when you forget a dentist appointment, blow by a deadline for turning in a report, or wind up frantically rushing around to set up at the last minute the party you scheduled weeks ago, the executive function weaknesses of poor working memory and insufficient motivation and effort are "running you." Too often, you are running after recurring problems in daily living when instead you could be containing and managing them internally so that they won't occur in the first place. In order to minimize and/or eliminate these unpleasant experiences, I cannot overstate how important it is for you to commit fully to valuing and developing the internal mental processes which guide and direct your behavior, including both the cooler cognitive functions as well as warmer, modulated adaptive emotions.

Okay, fine you say. But how do I do this? Give me examples of combining these elements that will not only allow me to understand the concepts better, but which also can serve as a template for devising other interventions. I am happy to oblige, and in keeping with the book's emphasis on using simple examples to illustrate complicated ideas, let's use two examples from everyday life: one which pertains to remembering a recurrent but intermittent commitment, and the second to devising and maintaining new daily rituals.

Repeat performances that stay the same

Let's start with the intermittent but recurrent event. You have some mature beautiful houseplants (a large, lush Boston fern, a healthy Christmas cactus that blooms every November and some assorted herbs you use for cooking). These plants are important to you decoratively, sentimentally and even financially (replacing herbs can get expensive). The plants get plenty of sunlight but when you forget to water them, the fern in particular can turn brown and the English thyme dries out and dies. Also, sometimes when you water, you often prune a bit to help their growth. They only need to be watered once or twice a week, so the task isn't onerous, it just requires some vigilance. What do you do to deal with this using hypothetical thinking and an antecedent mindset?

Relying on your capacity to think about non-present events and formulate if-then statements, start by imagining two scenarios. In the first, imagine your plants verdant and thriving because you're watering and pruning them regularly. Now the second scenario: you haven't watered in two weeks; brown fronds ring the base of the fern and the once bushy English thyme is pale in color and scraggly. Scenario one is what you want, but now you must engage your executive functions to develop words, images, motivation and thinking which will form your action steps. Analyze when you are most likely to have the bandwidth and motivation to water and prune. That could be Sunday morning, right after your run but before you pull *The New York Times* from its blue wrapper. Since you always make coffee  before your run, you could put your watering can or a picture of it by the coffee maker the night before. Next morning, you see it. Now you are pairing coffee with watering plants, thinking in words and images about each and feeling optimistic about keeping your plants healthy.

Now you have some key elements of an antecedent mindset in place but there is still a problem to overcome: time. You are formulating these steps on Tuesday, but it will be another five days before you implement the steps. How will you keep the goal and the steps front and center, keep them at the ready since thoughts in working memory fade over time? You resolve that each morning between now and Sunday, you will rehearse the steps of "watering plants on Sunday" in your head. In the past, you've dreaded these kind of minders, especially when they came from teachers or parents, but you find that it doesn't take much time to do it and it is satisfying to meet your own sub-goal. Maybe you have "externalized" your internal rehearsal of steps for a "To Do" list where you have written the steps down. Saturday evening arrives, you put a picture of the watering can by the coffee maker. On Sunday morning as you come in from your run, you grab a cup of coffee and, resisting the urge to pull the *Times* from its wrapper, execute your plant watering and pruning routine as you sip your coffee. Mission accomplished.

From here your challenge is to keep the protocol going. Obviously, you may need some external reminders (e.g., post-its or alerts on your smart phone) and you will also want to think about potential obstacles (e.g., You remember that you are scheduled to go hiking next Sunday.). That said, having scoped out all the steps, rehearsed and then executed them, the odds are the combination of goal accomplishment and felt sense of satisfaction will boost your motivation, and you will continue to water your plants regularly. But maintenance of the goal rests on maintaining the value you attach to hypothetical reasoning and to your capacity to adopt an antecedent mindset to develop action steps.

Generating a new action sequence: Specificity, flexibility and self-discipline

Let's move on to the second specific intervention: developing and maintaining a new ritual. Utilizing the plant watering example, this class of interventions involves more up-front effort and thinking because the actions are unknown to you as you begin the process. What do I mean? Well, with plant watering and pruning, you already know the steps (fill the watering can, water each plant, pluck off dead leaves or stems). But let's say you are having to devise an approach to a task or set of tasks which you don't really know how to do, or that have flummoxed you in the past. The latter situation is what Susan (the college freshman who binge-watched Netflix) faced when she switched majors and began attending a new college. She knew that dedicating set times for studying had always been a catch-as-catch-can affair for her, but now she was taking science classes in anatomy and physiology. She had more frequent homework assignments and tests than she had in her women's studies and film courses. Wisely, she had realized that she needed a major where the task structure of her assignments would be a better fit with her aptitudes and need for more frequent assignments and tests. Nevertheless, she still had to devise a particularized set of steps for managing her time so she would be prepared for class. The approach she generated combined changes in the where, when and what of her study habits. Specifically, the three elements can be summarized as follows:

1) **Where to study.** Susan decided to do most of her work on campus at the library because she knew she would be less likely to become distracted if she had driven to school and positioned herself in a place where others around her were studying.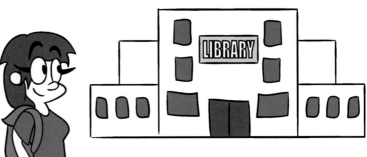

2) **When to study.** Susan decided to dedicate 2 hours just before her anatomy and physiology class to do the work due for that day or to study for any quizzes or tests. She imagined that giving herself a reasonable but limited time frame would help galvanize her motivation and reduce chances for distraction.

3) **What to study.** Reading and homework for anatomy/ physiology were the first tasks to accomplish. If she found she had additional time, Susan would work on reading or homework for her other courses.

Susan also wanted to change some other aspects of her daily routine (earlier bedtime, waking up earlier and exercising) and we used my variation of a behavior chart (IM Self Monitoring, described later in this chapter) to assist with charting her compliance.

Implementation of the new ritual began to yield positive results. Susan earned "A"s on anatomy and physiology tests and labs, and the instructor, noticing Susan's aptitude/ achievement, recommended her as a student tutor for the course. Realistic appraisals of her strengths and weaknesses, together with an increasing reliance on if-then thinking laid the foundation for devising not only an effective homework ritual, but also a regimen which provided daily affirmation of her ability to overcome executive function weaknesses. Episodes of flagging motivation, a problem which recurred from time-to-time, also diminished, particularly as Susan became the "in-demand" student tutor in the anatomy and physiology class.

We end the chapter with a cornerstone of pediatric mental health treatment: behavior management, its principles, common forms and some approaches I developed that "speak" directly to weaknesses with ADHD. Behavior management has been a staple in treatment for many types of childhood psychopathology and is nearly always part of a treatment plan for children with ADHD. Interestingly, however, I have found that methods most often used with children can be adapted for older adolescents and adults. And as with the antecedent mindset, the developmental edge conferred by age can be very helpful in terms of an adult's capacity to think about and execute behavior plans and strategies.

Behavior therapy, usually in the form of behavior charts and point systems, rests on the theory of operant conditioning. Originated and advanced by psychologist B.F. Skinner, a central tenet of operant conditioning is that behavior is "reinforced" by its consequences. Reinforcement refers to anything following the execution of a behavior which increases the probability that the behavior recurs. How does this apply to the "too much" or "too little" behavior associated with ADHD? Let's take a common example that is a composite of presenting concerns offered in my office. When I am beginning treatment with a family, I often ask about "morning routines;" i.e., the daily self-care behaviors that children need to do to get ready for school: getting out of bed and dressed; brushing teeth; organizing their homework, etc.

Morning routine behaviors are a behavioral therapist's near ideal opportunity to implement the theory of operant conditioning and reinforcement in real time. Why? The behaviors: 1) can be defined clearly; 2) are discrete; and 3) can be made time-specific in terms of when they occur and their duration. For most school-aged children, morning routines involve tasks which usually are age-appropriate for them. For children with behavior regulation problems, however, execution is often hit or miss and so any daily routines can be the source of great agitation for families.

A typical behavior chart is formatted with examples of "who, what, when" types of declarative statements, such as "Sam will brush his teeth every morning after breakfast." To set up a chart, the therapist first makes sure Sam knows how to perform all the elements of the behavior (e.g., toothpaste on brush, up and down motion in mouth) and then sets up a reinforcement for executing the behavior. Sam gets a "+" on his chart every time he engages in the behavior. As the "+s" accumulate, they can be turned in for material rewards (back-up reinforcers) that the child desires. In theory, the provision of a "reinforcement" (something Sam wants) should increase the probability that Sam will engage in regular teeth brushing.

STANDARD BEHAVIOR CHART

Target Behaviors:			Scores:		
1. Sam will brush teeth right after breakfast			+ Done - Not done		

Week of: _____

Target Behavior:	1	2	3	4	5
Monday	+				
Tuesday	--				
Wednesday	+				
Thursday	+				
Friday	--				
Saturday	+				
Sunday	--				

For his tangible reward, Sam elected to earn an extra 25¢ for each "+" level execution of the tooth brushing target behavior, an amount which will be added to his weekly allowance of $5.00. As evidenced on the chart above, Sam earned a "+" for 4 days out of 7, so this week he earned an extra $1.00 when Mom and Dad give him his allowance. Sounds good, right? Sam is using an intervention that has demonstrated efficacy in theory and research, an intervention which provides positive reinforcement that should increase the possibility that the target behavior will be executed the same way in the future.

Except for one problem--and it's a BIG problem. Neuroscience has shown that for individuals with ADHD, the reward centers of their brains can be somewhat sluggish in their operation. As such, the provision of reinforcements doesn't necessarily boost the probability of repeat execution of a given behavior in the same way as it might for an individual without this condition. What's more, assuming that the child can perform the behavior you are asking for, the problem at hand isn't necessarily one connected only to pure execution; rather it is a problem with the independence, consistency and quality of the target behavior execution. What might this mean for the use of standard behavior charts for ADHD patients?

Self-evaluation with feedback: Now we're talking behavior change

In my practice, what I've found is that traditional behavior charts really have not worked because they did not "speak to" or remediate the central nature of the child's problem: behavior regulation, not simply behavior execution. Returning to the example, we know that on any given day, Sam can and does brush his teeth in the prescribed way. The central problem for Sam (and his parents) is that he doesn't do it consistently (every day or most days, not just sometimes), independently (without a parent nagging), and competently (paying attention to the quality of what he is doing).

What's more, studies comparing individuals with and without ADHD show that when those with the condition became inattentive or distracted while completing tasks, they were less likely than individuals without ADHD to return and persist to completion. This suggested to me that individuals with this condition needed to incorporate the notion of ongoing self-monitoring into their behavior therapy protocols. It also suggested that they needed immediate feedback in order to know how they were doing with respect to hitting the marks for consistency, independence and work quality.

Based on this reasoning, I developed a different behavior chart system which incorporated elements shown below.[8] In brief, it works as follows. Instead of children earning "+" and "-" for target behavior execution, a child and an adult rate the target behavior execution using a "2, 1, 0" scale. "2" level behavior usually refers to executing the target behavior with no reminders and at a high quality level. "1" usually refers to executing the behavior with 2 or fewer reminders and acceptable quality. And "0" is "Try again," meaning the individual needs many reminders and showed poor quality of execution or that the target behavior was not completed.

IM SELF-MONITORING© CHART								
Target Behaviors: 1. Sam will brush teeth right after breakfast.			**Scores:** 2: No Reminders/Good Quality 1: Two or Fewer Reminders/Okay Quality 0: Try Again/Many Reminders/Weak Quality					
Week of: _____								
Target Behavior:	**1** Parent	Sam		**2**		**3**		**4**
Monday								
Tuesday								
Wednesday								
Thursday								
Friday								
Saturday								
Sunday								

Building self-awareness: The first step

Timeliness of ratings and child-then-parent sequencing of ratings is important if the goal is to increase awareness of how one is executing a task. First, the child rates himself right after performing the target behavior and then the parent rates the behavior. In the system, matches between child and parent replace "+" and "-" as reinforcement. Why?

8   Sutherland, F.C. (2008) "IM Self-Monitoring and Stop Strategy," unpublished text in Power Point presentation. (IM refers to my Integrated Model of ADHD Management, and the copyright applies only to the scoring standards for self-monitoring.)

Because the objective of the behavior therapy as implemented through the chart is to nudge the child cognitively to practice being attentive to how they are executing a given target behavior, not simply whether they did it. And the child's also paying attention to the "how" in a particular way: "how independent was I and what was the quality of what I did?"

Returning to the "Sam" example, this is how Sam's chart might work if he did an excellent job of teeth brushing on Monday. (Sam's rating is in the shaded side of the chart and the parent's is in the unshaded side.)

IM SELF-MONITORING© CHART						
Target Behaviors: 1. Sam will brush teeth right after breakfast.		**Scores:** 2: No Reminders/Good Quality 1: Two or Fewer Reminders/Okay Quality 0: Try Again/Many Reminders/Weak Quality				
Week of: _____						
Target Behavior:	**1** Parent Sam		**2**	**3**	**4**	
Monday	2	2				
Tuesday						
Wednesday						
Thursday						
Friday						
Saturday						
Sunday						

Monday's matching pairs of "2s" tell us a couple of things about how Sam fared on his teeth brushing goal. First, his self-monitoring score of "2" (in the shaded side of the box) indicates that not only did he execute the task, but also in his mind, he did it without being reminded and with good quality. Presumably, he was monitoring those two aspects of the task as he was executing them. But in order for Sam to truly know whether he stayed the course in terms of independent task persistence and high quality of work, he needs feedback from someone who was also watching his task execution as it was unfolding.

Needing feedback brings us to the second aspect of the system--a check on one's self-appraisal. Sam's parent evaluated his task execution in the same way as Sam did. Therefore the pair of "2s" also indicates that Sam brushed his teeth well without reminders.

IM SELF-MONITORING© CHART						
Target Behaviors: 1. Sam will brush teeth right after breakfast.			**Scores:** 2: No Reminders/Good Quality 1: Two or Fewer Reminders/Okay Quality 0: Try Again/Many Reminders/Weak Quality			
Week of: _____						
Target Behavior:	**1** Parent	Sam	**2**	**3**	**4**	
Monday	2	2				
Tuesday	2	2				
Wednesday	0	2				
Thursday	1	1				
Friday						
Saturday						
Sunday						

Let's move on to Sam's second self-monitoring chart, as shown above. Now we see four days of ratings. Tuesday's matching "2s" convey the same picture of the tooth brushing target that we saw on Monday. No reminders, high quality and, most importantly, agreement between Sam and parent as to how he did the task. Wednesday was a different day. On that morning, Sam was building with Legos when it came time to brush his teeth, and when he finally did separate from the Legos, his mother already had asked him four times to do so. Also, Sam forgot to put toothpaste on his brush because he was rushing to get to the bus on time. Moreover, Sam scribbled a "2" on his chart for Wednesday, but Mom gave him a "0". Sam was not pleased, but later he and his mom talked about why he earned the "0"--four reminders and poor quality. On Thursday, Sam was running late again for the bus, but he did manage to brush his teeth independently. The quality, however, was not great (not long enough). Sam gave himself a "1", as did Mom.

An essential point of taking you through this exercise (one that I have gone through with kids and parents many times) is to underscore just how difficult it is for individuals with ADHD to make changes in their behavior that translate into true control. Most kids can execute a behavior such as brushing their teeth on a given day, but that fact in and of itself says little-to-nothing about their ability to regulate and monitor their behavior over several days. In order to do that, the behavior system they use needs to address their problems with evaluating and monitoring the tasks they execute. The ultimate goal is two-fold: to allow them to perform tasks independently with good quality and to be consistently receptive to feedback.

Internalizing feedback: Putting the brakes on the same old, same old

For individuals with ADHD, the importance of in-the-moment feedback cannot be overstated. Without it, these individuals can become truly handicapped in terms of adjusting their behavior to fit the demands of their lives. Without access to and internalization of feedback, individuals with ADHD are consigned to operate in life with limited awareness of how they did something. Moreover, when their behavior falls short of meeting a goal, figuring out why it happened, without feedback, can feel next to impossible. But, going deeper into the neuroscience, we can ask why? I contend that part of the answer lies in reflecting on the nature of the condition, as described in Chapter 2.

Recall that with the growth and development of executive functions, individuals gain mastery over their ability to guide and direct behavior. But if the development of those functions is continually being compromised by ADHD, then of course it makes sense that these individuals' capacities to monitor themselves will be weaker than that of their peers. Now also consider that part of what allows executive functions to grow and develop is the shaping they receive from interaction with the outside world. Unfortunately, though, because ADHD also impairs reception of input from the outside world, the full apprehension and benefits of that input is not internalized in the same way as it would be for someone who does not have this condition. The upshot is that lags in development are compounded by insensitivity to feedback resulting in real time problems with task execution. Specifically, task execution is ineffective or incomplete in part because past experience is not used well to shape it. Basically what unfolds repeatedly is someone tied unproductively to their current circumstances, sometimes referred to as a "prisoner of the immediate" or a "prisoner of the now."

In my office, patients sometimes describe the aforementioned problems with prospective and retrospective thinking as a sense of being "fuzzy" about the particulars of tasks to be done or of those just completed. They report frustration when they are unable to recall important aspects of recently executed tasks. And especially when they are explaining complete "ball drops,"[9] these patients report feelings of shame, anger and regret as well as a palpable sense that their self confidence has been shaken yet again. Listening to and thinking about their accounts helped me recognize why in-the-moment feedback is not only helpful but also essential. Such feedback pushes the individual to link important information about task execution with mental processes they will need to perform the same task in the future. In order for lasting behavior change to occur, tight timing is needed between outside feedback and the mental shifts necessary for task execution.

Listen to how Beth, a sophomore in college with ADHD described the importance of feedback when she was a senior in high school:

"It took me a long time to realize that rather than avoiding feedback about something that was difficult (like some types of school work), what I actually needed to do was to embrace feedback about the task I found difficult. Only then could I create ways to do things better in the future, and figure out ways to keep myself motivated and focused in the moment even when I knew a task had the potential to be really boring."

---

9   Ball drop is the term we use to describe failing or forgetting to do something you had needed or committed to do.

While my IM Self-Monitoring system is directed at improving independent compliance and self-awareness about task execution, the principal target of STOP Strategy© is disruptive emotional impulsivity. Given that the speed with which emotions are experienced and then expressed by individuals with ADHD, STOP Strategy© is intended to provide "mental breathing room" for cooler executive functions and memory retrieval, both of which allow for more adaptive responses. STOP was designed to support not only the immediate de-escalation and inhibition of hot emotions such as anger or panic, but also to maintain emotional control when circumstances are becoming too negative, anxiety-ridden or exciting.

Think back to Barkley's model of ADHD and recall what is required to accomplish a desired goal. It requires creating mental breathing room by inhibiting an immediate response and maintaining a delay in responding. Add to that Barkley's view that emotional expression is part and parcel of any person's behavior.

Now think about this model in the context of everyday life. Say you are driving to work on a busy road during the early morning rush hour and it is raining. People are in a hurry, visibility is reduced and other drivers might be more stressed or irritable than normal. At the same time, you want to get to work safely; that is your goal. You move into the left lane in preparation to make a left turn at an intersection where there is no light and a great deal of oncoming traffic. You look in your rearview mirror and notice the driver behind you is getting visibly upset that you are interfering with his forward motion. Unfortunately, you can't do anything but wait until it feels safe to you to make the left turn. In this situation, you must inhibit an immediate response to turn quickly to get away from this guy. If you lose control over your inhibition and fail to let your executive functions operate, the goal of getting to work safely and calmly could be compromised.

Given that inhibiting fast hot emotions is a prerequisite for accessing cooler executive functions, it follows that with ADHD youngsters, one must intervene before the emerging emotion disrupts behavior. Waiting until a child is yelling, crying, or hysterically laughing and then applying a consequence to arrest the immediate response (much less discourage future problems) just doesn't make sense. Rather, one needs to catch the emotion as it is beginning to unfold and halt it in its tracks. In order to do this, parents and child must practice in low stress conditions the de-escalation process so that when the high-stress moment presents itself, they can work together to keep hot emotions in check.

In a situation where unregulated emotion threatens to upend adaptive functioning, there are two objectives for using a STOP. First, it creates a sustained delay in responding that provides an opportunity for a more adaptive response to be formulated. During the delay, for example, executive functions can be accessed and utilized to shape a response that is better suited to the existing circumstances (Think of the driving example I just gave you.) Second, imposing a STOP can prevent escalations of yelling (what behavior therapists call negative reinforcement spirals) by arresting the immediate conflict between parent and child.

So how does STOP work? Imagine that a child and adult are beginning to experience conflict or too much excitement with one another. Before the situation gets too heated, the adult calls upon the child to take a STOP. In its purest form, both the child and the adult will stop moving and talking until the heated or excited emotion has receded. Once both the child and the adult have regained emotional control (as demonstrated by both of them being able to talk to one another about the trigger issue without becoming heated or excited), then they can resume talking for the purposes of problem-solving. Or, if the trigger issue no longer seems important, they can simply move on. Practically what this means is that adults and children agree in advance of heated exchanges to take STOPs as things are starting to get too "hot" or too exciting in order to protect the good feeling and team work they need to function well together. In my practice, we discuss past episodes of arguments and talk about the consequences (usually unsatisfactory for everyone). These discussions form the basis for wanting to pivot to a different approach.

Once the ground work is laid, we practice taking a STOP or two in the session (there is no conflict–I just call a STOP and everyone stops moving and talking). I also ask that families keep a STOP log in a simple spiral notebook that tracks the STOPs taken during the period between therapy sessions. In the STOP log, families are asked to write a series of bullet points as follows: 1) What triggered the need for a STOP? 2) Were all members able to get into STOP mode? If not, what happened? 3) How long did the STOP take? 4) How did the STOP end? Did members talk about what had happened? Was their restitution in the form of an apology or help in making up for the lost time, or did people just move on to other activities because what had occurred wasn't important enough to "process" any further?

STOP is like Time-out with a twist

The origins of STOP were derived from the well-known behavior therapy technique known as "Time-out," which I expanded to address not only behavioral inhibition but also two structural family therapy issues: specifically preserving hierarchy in the executive subsystem and maintenance of clear boundaries. I will define hierarchy and boundaries in detail in Chapter 4, but for the moment let me explain how parental authority operates in the context of implementing the intervention. First, adults are in charge of setting up and practicing STOP strategy in advance of situations where it might be needed. If in real life a child refuses to comply with a STOP when instructed, the adults maintain their STOP and refuse to give the child attention or involvement until the child complies with the STOP directive. Second, STOPs are initiated by adults when conflict or excitement is beginning to escalate, not after an activity has been fully upended. Early intervention in a situation protects the adults' authority by preserving their emotional control. Third, STOP immediately thwarts the slide into maladaptive communication patterns that interfere with parents being able to provide clear directives in a more neutral, collaborative fashion.

STOP is framed to the adult and the child as a collaborative, shared activity – adult and child are a team and their joint goal is to keep conflict or excitement from interfering with accomplishing whatever they are doing together. The intention is to block the back and forth argument and replace it with an emotional climate where cooler heads can prevail.

I'm not suggesting the process is easy. To be sure, while I may frame STOP to families as a collaborative activity, parents and especially adolescents struggle mightily to make the intervention work in real time, even after considerable repetition and practice. Listen to what Terry, a verbally adept attorney, had to say after a particularly rough STOP with her daughter Kate.

"Kate kept following me around the house spewing nasty comments, trying to get me to respond to her even though I knew I needed to get away from her so that she would stop talking. Finally I went into my walk-in closet and closed the door in order to force myself to take a STOP. Kate kept yelling at me, but I was determined not to be baited by her and pulled into a fight."

For readers familiar with child management techniques, they will recognize that STOP shares a key similarity with Time-out. In Time-out, a child who violates a rule is placed in a chair for a certain number of minutes, thus removing him from desired activities and adult attention and involvement. Both Time–out and STOP share that approach as a way of increasing the probability that the child will not engage in the offending behavior again.

Now, while STOP shares with Time-out the "removal feature" of punishment, it also modifies the punishment component somewhat by supporting (or what I call "pulling for") adult/child collaboration in accomplishing the joint goal of keeping conflict or excitement in check. I created this modification because I wanted the intervention to support the maintenance of emotional neutrality and collaboration in both child and parent even as it sought to "punish" maladaptive responses on the part of the child.

Car rides are a perfect time to practice STOP

To illustrate how STOP "pulls for" collaboration between parent and child, consider a common, real-life example. Dad is driving with two siblings in the back seat on a trip to a desired activity. The siblings must sit near one another sharing desired hand-held video games, books or other activities. Let's assume Dad has used STOP strategy in the past. Further, while getting in the car, he reminds the kids about expected good car behavior (e.g., sharing of activities) and may ask the siblings to list other non-negotiable behaviors (e.g., no arguing). Dad may even ask the kids to "role play" what they will do if he has to cue them if their voices are getting too loud or they are beginning to argue. These steps prior to the trip are a key component of the collaborative aspect of STOP, because they underscore what kids need to do to make the car ride a success. Sometimes, however, despite the best planning, kids will begin to misbehave, and Dad's pre-set cues don't end the conflict. Now it's time for the "punishment" side of STOP. After Dad calls "STOP," he stops the car and all communication with the kids. Nothing happens until both kids get themselves into STOP, meaning that yelling or arguing has stopped and the kids are sitting quietly. Only then does Dad determine whether the outing can continue. By refusing to engage with the kids until they "separate" from one another (verbally and physically), the parent is able to retain control and potentially salvage the outing.

For almost anyone, behavior change is always difficult. But as I've tried to demonstrate, it is monumentally difficult for individuals with some combination of inhibitory delays constitutionally-based low motivation, time management problems, and insensitivity to feedback. That said, for these individuals change is achievable, but it literally can take a lifetime.

CHAPTER 4
ADHD and Family Dynamics:
Ready or not, everybody's impacted

Treatment of a child or adolescent does not occur in a vacuum. It happens within the jumbled reality of family life. Add to that the high probability that a parent or sibling may also be coping with the condition and you have the potential for (as one mother in my practice is fond of saying) "one hot mess."

In keeping with the goal of providing an accessible but theoretically-driven formulation of ADHD and family dynamics, here is a brief historical overview and summary of some central elements of child and family treatment. Since I relied on structural family therapy in developing the IM model of ADHD management, key concepts of the therapy will be explained as succinctly as possible. Then we'll circle back and link up those elements with management of ADHD.

Historical Background

For decades, the role played by family members, particularly parents, in the mental health treatment of their children and adolescents has varied greatly depending on the theoretical orientation of the therapist. Psychoanalytically-trained child therapists worked in play settings, seeing parents only for separate consultations. Given the tenets of psychoanalysis, in the backdrop of those visits was the assumption that glitches in a child's progression through psychosexual stages provided the basis for child adjustment problems, from social anxiety to aggressive behavior to (most famously) toileting problems (e.g., Freud's anal stage). The clear implication was that the source of the child's problem had to do with his relationship with his parents.[10]

The psychoanalytic approach began to be challenged in the 1970's with the family therapy movement. Structural family therapy practitioners such as Salvador Minuchin at the Philadelphia Child Guidance Clinic upended not only conventional notions about how therapy should be conducted (e.g., observing sessions through one-way mirror vs. the sanctum sanctorum of totally private sessions between patient and therapist) but also, crucially, how and why psychopathology emerges in children and adolescents. Breaking from the traditional psychoanalytic focus on an individual's internal conflicts as the source of psychopathology, Minuchin advanced the notion that an individual's overall mental health is tied directly to family interactions, or what he called the "transactional patterns" operating in real time within a family.

---

10   Per toileting problems, parents' expectations may have been too demanding in toddlerhood, leading the child to control when and how he would move his bowels usually in the form of "accidents."

Hierarchy, boundaries and other factors

Minuchin maintained that family interactions are influenced by variables that impact the family structure. One variable he called "hierarchy" refers to the power arrangements in families where parents and children have different levels of authority and where parental teamwork establishes rules and routines that govern family life. A hierarchy also is comprised of subsystems, which most commonly include an executive subsystem (parents) and a sibling subsystem (their kids). In *Families and Family Therapy*, Minuchin offered the following diagram of a single-mother household, as shown below.

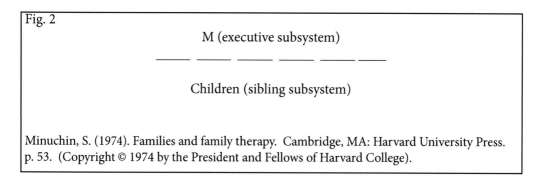

Fig. 2

M (executive subsystem)

——— ———— ———— ———— ———— ————

Children (sibling subsystem)

Minuchin, S. (1974). Families and family therapy. Cambridge, MA: Harvard University Press. p. 53. (Copyright © 1974 by the President and Fellows of Harvard College).

In this diagram, Minuchin is portraying a functional hierarchy, with M (executive system, in this case Mother) having appropriate authority over the children (sibling subsystem). The dashed line represents a clear boundary, meaning that M communicates definitively the rules the children are to follow. Minuchin provides this example: "...the boundary of a parental subsystem is defined when a mother (M) tells her older child, 'You aren't your brother's parent. If he is riding in the street, tell me and I will stop him.'" (p. 53)

Here is a cartoon representation of a functional hierarchy modeled on Minuchin's example:

To be sure, different hierarchies influence how family members speak to one another. For example, adults are more inclined to tolerate criticism coming from one another than they would be if it were coming from a child. Also within a family hierarchy, mutual expectations of one another develop over time, and tensions build when a member repeatedly fails to live up to a shared expectation.

As Minuchin studied interfamily communication, he also identified a second variable affecting families that he called "boundaries." Boundaries

are the rules defining the "who and how" of participation between family members. An illustration of boundaries might be the following: a mother communicating more with her eldest child regarding responsibility-taking than she would with her youngest child, or fathers and mothers discussing family finances only with one another and not with their children. Who gets talked to about what topics, and how often that occurs – that, in a nutshell, is the concept of boundaries.

Family boundaries tend to be one of three types: clear, diffuse or rigid. As shown below, a clear boundary is a desirable form of communication between subsystems because it allows for the accomplishment of directives, while permitting family members to maintain their individuality and differentiation from one another. Preserving individuality and a healthy level of separateness is the key idea.

When boundaries are diffuse, parents and children engage frequently, but not necessarily constructively, often resulting in stress and discord. A family with communication characterized by diffuse boundaries is referred to as "enmeshed." Enmeshment is what it sounds like, people "on top of one another" with frequent directives often increasing the probability of conflict and a negative tone in a family. (It's the family communication pattern I frequently see in families with members who have ADHD.)

Conversely, rigid boundaries occur when communication is infrequent and/or disinterested. When a family has a lot of rigid boundaries, it is said to be characterized by "disengagement." And by this, Minuchin doesn't mean an over-controlling or rigid parenting style. Instead, it refers to an impermeable communication boundary, meaning that parents and kids cannot communicate effectively with one another. With disengaged families, it can take a 911-type emergency to get individuals to communicate and mobilize around an adverse event.

Here's Minuchin's rendering of the three types of boundaries:

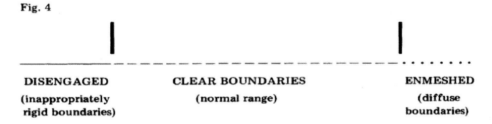

Fig. 4

DISENGAGED	CLEAR BOUNDARIES	ENMESHED
(inappropriately rigid boundaries)	(normal range)	(diffuse boundaries)

Minuchin, S. (1974). Families and family therapy. Cambridge, MA: Harvard University Press. p. 54. (Copyright © 1974 by the President and Fellows of Harvard College).

And here's a cartoon created to depict the three types of boundaries:

In addition to hierarchies and boundaries, Minuchin identified another set of forces or influences affecting a family interaction. These include family structure (two parents or single parent?), its stage of development (just married with young children or grandparents now raising grandchildren?), and, critically, the family's ability to adapt to changed circumstances such as a child developing a chronic health problem.

Relationship to mental health

As Minuchin and his colleagues watched and worked with various types of families over time, they concluded that adjustment problems in children developed from commonly recurring transactional patterns in the family (i.e., how family members interact with one another in real time). Going a step further, Minuchin contended that adjustment problems in children and adolescents were the result of particular types of interaction patterns. He observed these patterns across a variety of families with children manifesting different types of psychiatric disorders (e.g., anorexia, oppositional behavior, school phobia, etc.).

For Minuchin et al., gone were the assumptions about internal conflicts tied to psychosexual stages and a focus on past events as the source of current problems. What remained was the notion that parents were central to the expression of symptoms in their offspring. Real-time interactions between parents and children were deemed to be the principal "driver" of adjustment problems. Of particular importance were: 1) the nature of the interactions, meaning how directive, emotionally intrusive or controlling the communications were; and 2) the frequency of these types of communications, meaning did they occur many times around issues both large and small, or were they more directive and intrusive and occurring relatively infrequently.

Hierarchy, boundaries and ADHD

As I worked with families where ADHD was the primary presenting complaint, a pattern among hierarchy, boundaries and ADHD kept emerging: it was enmeshment with an affective tone of negativity and conflict. Hour after hour, I would take notes while listening to case histories of parents frustrated, angry and worried about their son or daughter with examples of "too much behavior" and/or "too little initiation and effort." These families began their days with conflict with one or both parents giving increasingly strident directives to get out of bed, get dressed, eat breakfast, refrain from playing video games, and so on.

I would respond with interventions intended to help structure and streamline the "must do tasks" of daily life. But no amount of distraction removal (including the morning cardinal rule: No TV) and advance planning (backpacks packed the night before) could compensate for what I came to realize was a structural problem in the family. Moreover, it became apparent that parents were "stuck conceptually" trying to correct lapses in the child's behavior through directives (ever more frequent, specific and hostile in tone). Why? Because the behavior lapses stemmed from neurodevelopmental delays, factors which directives alone were not going to correct. I began to see that if parents had a clear sense of how a child's ADHD predisposes the family to disordered dynamics, they could intelligently adopt more adaptive stances around their child's or adolescent's difficulties.

ADHD and family dynamics

The typical family in my practice has two parents with (in Minuchin-speak) a parent subsystem and a sibling subsystem and fairly predictable transactional patterns. As such, the parents are the "de facto" authority figures in charge of setting rules and routines that govern family life. While grandparents or other caregivers may be participating in child care, few if any lived with the nuclear family. So in terms of their most fundamental, readily apparent characteristics, nearly all the families I was seeing could fairly be described as "functional hierarchies."

Boundaries, however, were a different story. Specifically, boundaries (i.e., the rules and habits governing communication) were often compromised by a son or daughter with ADHD. Moreover, the trouble would grow steadily as the parent repeatedly gave directives without compliance from the affected child. Additionally, the increasing age of the "noncompliant" child would also contribute to family conflict because parents understandably would feel that an older child (e.g., 7 years of age) should be able to dress himself, especially if his 5-year-old sibling was already doing it somewhat independently. In sum, I saw that noncompliant behavior interfered repeatedly with the ADHD child's ability to live comfortably with siblings and that this behavior often extended to other settings, such as disrupting play dates or family gatherings.

Evaluating the boundaries in families with ADHD children or adolescents, I came to the following conclusion: enmeshment governed far too many interactions in families with a child or adolescent with ADHD, and the impact constricted the development of healthy autonomy and differentiation not just for the child but for the parents as well. That said, in the same family with a sibling without ADHD, communication patterns could approximate the standard of clear boundaries with appropriate levels of autonomy and differentiation, except when the unaffected sibling was drawn into unproductive exchanges triggered by the child with ADHD.

The following two cartoons depicting interactions between parents and two brothers (Kevin who has ADHD and Scott who does not) convey just how different the boundaries can be with each child. To manage the recurring disruptions with a child like Kevin, parents often try to correct the situation by delivering more directives ever more succinctly and by taking good parenting steps, such as making eye contact with the child before delivering the directive. Invariably, though, as the communications became more frequent and pointed, the affective tone can turn negative (what in structural family therapy parlance is referred to as "hostile enmeshment"). At the same time, in dealing with Scott, parents often experience a duality where Scott can follow a direction (with or without a reminder) and even remember to do things without being asked.

The daily stress of non-compliance with Kevin and the negative impact it has on Scott invariably leads parents to breaking points. Even when the severity of the condition is mild, the "scope" problem associated with ADHD makes it nearly impossible to approach the goal of clear boundaries and a neutral collaborative tone which characterizes adaptive parent-child communication. And for those parents with age-proximate siblings without ADHD, the difference in communication patterns is stark and upsetting.

Parents caught in a no-win situation

The following cartoons depict the odd split-screen experiences the parents have with Kevin and Scott, and the inevitable conflict that could unfold between the two brothers. Naturally, parents worry about the impact but would be at a loss as what to do about it.

The predicament of Kevin, Scott and their parents has emerged at times in my practice. Kathy is a physician and mother of two children born roughly two years apart. Her elder son Max has problems with emotional regulation and compliance consistent with his diagnosis of ADHD. His brother Alex is not affected by the condition and generally navigates his way through daily life without problems. Listen to Kathy's anguish over repeat interactions with Max characterized by hostile enmeshment.

"I know that when I really start yelling at Max for not getting out to the bus stop on time, I'm losing some of my legitimate authority and influence as a parent. It's just so difficult when simple requests like "put your coat on" work with Alex but not for Max. I do understand that it's truly harder for Max to hold on to a direction and follow-through without complaint, but sometimes I just "lose it." I can't help it; I want it to be easy, the way it is with Alex.

And while it may hardly seem like a benefit, Kathy is fortunate because at least she has a sophisticated understanding of ADHD that allows her to appreciate why Max can have recurrent problems with the simplest of tasks.

Mornings with Scott are so easy! He can get ready by himself!

Today's Recap:

I know! He also remembers to do his chores!

Kevin was such a pain this morning! He was moving so slowly!

Today's Recap:

I had to remind him to take out the trash four times today, he still hasn't done it!

Watching them fight isn't helping anyone! It just makes it worse!

Today's Recap:

Kevin, just do what Mom and Dad ask you to do.

How should we deal with this? We can't have this going on forever!

63

Not the case for many parents whose children receive this diagnosis with little information about the condition and the "scope problem" associated with it.

How to think about boundary problems

Absent a diagnosis that explains the condition accurately and thoroughly, a parent is "set up" to misattribute the reasons for why his/her child is behaving this way. Invariably, blame can start flying in all directions, particularly if one parent is spending more time engaged in the daily management of the child with ADHD. But this is where referencing Minuchin's thinking can be so helpful. Recall that the desirable form of parent-child communication is one characterized by clear boundaries. Why? As I noted earlier, clear boundaries allow for the "accomplishment of directives while permitting individuals to maintain their individuality and differentiation from one another." Obviously, developmental considerations play a role in how much autonomy can be expected, but by emphasizing just how essential it is for parents and children to become differentiated from one another, Minuchin's theory gave researchers and clinicians a powerful tool to inform their understanding of childhood psychopathology.

A child with a behavior regulation problem turns parents into "sitting ducks," likely to be lured into recurrent patterns of enmeshment that are well-intended but ultimately lead to chronic family conflict. To make matters worse, the conflict is divisive, leaving parents blaming one another about why child X is behaving this way. "Dad is too lenient." "Mother is too strict." "We don't enforce house rules consistently." "House rules are too overbearing and burdensome; our house operates like an institution, not a loving home."

While the solutions to effective management will be created and modified frequently over the course of a child's life, I found that unless and until parents had a full picture of their predicament, they were at risk for underestimating and misattributing what they should do for and with each other in order to support their child.

It's time for a conceptual shift

For starters, parents need to give up the notion that they themselves can "correct" a neurodevelopmental delay through directives alone. Rather, if they are going to move into a space of clear boundaries with a neutral and collaborative affective tone, everyone (but especially the parents) also needs to adopt realistic expectations. Here are a few key ideas:

1) As much as possible, allow an antecedent mindset to permeate how you structure your life with your child. You will be less likely to become overbearingly directive if you, your spouse, your child and their siblings think together to plan and shape how you want an event to unfold.

2) As is developmentally appropriate, get the child involved in building their executive functions by following what I call a "You either run this or it runs you" doctrine. It is vital for a parent to get clear about whose developmental delay this is and proceed in a

manner which seeks to restore and preserve everybody's autonomy. Also, promoting differentiation has a positive impact on emotional tone in the household, because the burden of the parent having to change the child's behavior has been eased. Now the goal is figuring out how we can work together as a team to accomplish whatever it is we need to do. Each member of the team has a part to play, one that is both coordinated with but also distinct from that of another family member.

3) When family relations start to become tense and in danger of reverting back to enmeshment, observe this and remind family members what is happening. (Pull out the "Boundaries" cartoons found earlier in this chapter.) Knowledge truly is power in these circumstances. You must summon the inhibitory control to realize that as a family you are allowing yourselves to regress. This knowledge should be the springboard to getting yourselves back on track.

4) As one parent may also have ADHD, he or she can take the lead in modeling how to avoid unproductive interactions by using behavior change techniques (antecedent mindset, IM self-monitoring, STOP) for his/her family members.

Tackling enmeshment: Daughter as CEO of the Twits Corporation

One of the most rewarding aspects of my practice occurs when families pick up on a concept and use it to shape an approach. One of the more ingenious examples of this occurred late one Friday afternoon while I was meeting with a 20-year-old daughter, who was living at home, and her two parents. After trying college, both residential and commuting from home, this young woman had decided that in order to become a more autonomous adult, she needed to live in a group setting that focused on teaching independent living skills to young adults. This was a kind of watershed moment that came as a surprise to her parents, but to which they responded with interest and suspension of judgment. While there were momentary flashes of what could have become enmeshed interactions at home, I pointed out what I was seeing and everyone pulled back.

What followed in the balance of the session was remarkable. I will summarize it here. The parents are Nate and Julie; their daughter's name is Megan.

To his daughter Nate said, "Okay. Dr. Sutherland was talking about us being a team as we try to figure out this life skills program you are interested in. Mommy and I don't want to get into a pattern of reminding or nagging you to investigate it, so let's pretend that you are the CEO of a corporation, our corporation. We'll call it the Twits Corporation. Now Megan, you assign each of us jobs as to what you would like us to do to help you explore this."

The exercise pushed Megan to think about what she actually needed to start this process and what each of us could provide. From Nate, Megan learned that he had a friend who was familiar with services for individuals with disabilities. Megan asked me to consult my professional colleagues. (I actually was planning to speak with an executive director of a private program for young adults.) Megan asked her mother Julie for help organizing the material into a binder so we could review it. Finally, Megan assigned herself the job of searching for possible programs on line.

ADHD in the family: No quick fixes

It would be a mistake to end this chapter with readers thinking that once adaptive family dynamics are set in motion, they always stick and life is good. NO, far from it. Old challenges are replaced with new ones when families are dealing with a condition as pervasive as ADHD. However, when armed with concepts that help explain why strained dynamics keep occurring, parents and their kids are in a far better position to construct ways to redirect themselves without the judgment and blame that make reconciliation and collaboration so difficult to achieve.

CHAPTER 5
Patients' Perspectives on Medication:
What it does and does not provide

If setting off brushfires of debate and controversy appeals to you, go ahead and take a position for or against the use of stimulant medication to treat ADHD. While these medications have been researched for decades, the science (both pro and con), which ideally should inform the general public's view of stimulants, never attracts the same spotlight as does the white hot intensity of personal opinion.

The strong reactions are not surprising. The recurrent use of any medication can become a heated topic, and it often comes down to personal viewpoints. For general medical conditions, some use drugs liberally when acutely or chronically ill; others rarely use them. I'm in the latter camp, sometimes to the detriment of my comfort or recovery time. With respect to medications to treat ADHD, I also understand that some people will react and speak out without sufficient understanding of what neuroscience has taught us about stimulants (their mechanisms of action, benefits, side-effects, etc.). They are moved more by personal experience that informs and, yes, biases their opinions.

Carte blanche denunciations of stimulant medication have always made me uneasy. As someone who has worked in the pediatric mental health field for decades, I find that these medications, properly used, can help to improve the behavior and academic achievement of children and adolescents with bona fide ADHD. Stimulants can help these young people curb impulsivity and sustain attention so that they can function better in both social and academic contexts. The same argument can be applied to adults with properly diagnosed ADHD.

That said, however, stimulant medication is not a panacea. (With a condition as complex as ADHD affecting so many aspects of a person's behavior regulation, how could it be otherwise?) Rather, medication is just one part of the treatment regimen, all of which also includes education about the condition, psychotherapy, tutoring and coordination between the key players in a child's life (including parents, teachers, academic tutors, physicians and mental health practitioners).

Adding patients' perspectives to the decision-making process

For those of you who are newly diagnosed with ADHD (or those who are parents of children with an ADHD diagnosis), considering a trial of medication is a big decision. Fortunately, there are resources that can help in making an informed choice. These include consulting with trusted mental health professionals, reading literature informed by reputable scientific sources and then weighing the possible benefits and risks of stimulant use. (To assist with the "reading" component, I have included a short list of publications in the List of Resources at the end of the book.)

But where else can you turn for information?

I believe that perhaps one of the most valuable perspectives on medication use goes largely untapped. What is it? Put simply, it's the viewpoint of a patient with properly diagnosed ADHD who takes stimulants to manage their symptoms. You will hear several of these perspectives later in the chapter.

How did I get here?

The catalyst for my thinking was motivated by a critic of stimulant medication for the treatment of ADHD. In a *New York Times Sunday Review* article (published January 28, 2012), L. Allan Sroufe, an emeritus psychology professor at the University of Minnesota, refuted the efficacy of stimulant medication to provide lasting benefits in learning and behavior. He argued that the basis for using such medications--namely, problems with concentration and attention were due to brain problems, either genetic or in-born-- was flawed.[11] He concluded that using stimulant medication to treat the academic and behavioral problems arising from attention-deficit disorder is mistaken because as he stated, "Putting children on drugs does nothing to change the conditions that derail their development in the first place." (p. 3)

Reading Dr. Sroufe's argument fired me up, and I decided to put together an article critiquing the views he had advanced. Below is an excerpt:[12]

"While evidence challenging Dr. Sroufe's position could surely be summoned from various academic quarters (psychiatry, neuropsychology and genetics, among others), I was struck by an omission in his piece that seemed both obvious and necessary in any debate about stimulant medication: the perspective of the patient who takes them regularly to manage the symptoms of attention-deficit disorder. Patients who have taken these medications, sometimes for years, could provide useful information regarding the impact the drugs have had on their long term functioning, both the benefits and the drawbacks. While children, by dint of their cognitive developmental status, would not be good candidates to interview on their present and past functioning, I thought that adolescents, who have the capacity to think about non-present events such as their past lives as children, could provide important insights about stimulant use.

As a psychologist who has worked for more than twenty years with children, adolescents and their families, I have participated in the management of children with developmental delays (learning disabilities, attention-deficit disorder) over extended time periods. With this in mind, I selected three individuals who were willing to provide some 'real

11   Dr. Sroufe noted that subsequent research, which initially had indicated improvements in behavior and academic functioning while taking stimulant medication, failed to provide convincing evidence of benefit over time. Dr. Sroufe also cited research showing that the environment of the child predicted the development of attention-deficit disorder, not measures of neurological anomalies at birth, IQ, nor infant temperament (including infant activity).

12   Sutherland, F.C. (2012) "Stimulants and Attention-Deficit Disorder, Three Perspectives," unpublished manuscript.

world' perspectives on the role that stimulant medication has played in the treatment of attention-deficit disorder. Let me be clear; my intent was not to 'lead the witnesses' into personal testimonies that amount to nothing more than endorsements of stimulant medication. Rather I wanted to provide readers with a window into what it is like to have this condition and to use these medications on a regular basis."

One of my major objectives was to get at the before-and-after experience of taking stimulant medication, particularly in a school setting, and how it impacted learning. I also addressed questions surrounding the "costs" of medication (i.e., side effects), the benefits, and whether changes in environment alone would have produced significant improvements. Finally, I asked the interviewees about their opinions regarding Dr. Sroufe's points that stimulants produce only short term benefits and that ADHD is more the result of experiential/environmental variables than constitutional ones. In all three cases, the adolescents were receiving other types of support (e.g., tutoring, accommodations in school, psychotherapy), in addition to stimulant medication to manage the academic and behavioral issues associated with attention-deficit disorder.

Here is some background about each interviewee (taken from the original article):

"Amy is a high school senior with Attention-Deficit/Hyperactivity Disorder, Combined Type and mild learning disabilities in language-based subjects (foreign language, written expression). She was diagnosed with ADHD in second grade and has been taking stimulant medication daily since age eight. Educated in private schools, Amy participated in regular education classes throughout her entire school career. Outside of school, she received tutoring support for academic subjects and study skills. She has maintained an 'A' average this year, and she will be attending a small liberal arts college in the fall. I have worked with Amy and her family on and off for 10 years."

"Beth is a high school sophomore who was formally diagnosed 18 months ago with Attention- Deficit/Hyperactivity Disorder, Inattentive Type and began taking stimulant medication shortly after the diagnosis was made. She has attended a private school for her entire academic career. Academic difficulties and underachievement in middle school led Beth and her parents to seek evaluation and treatment. Beth and her parents have been participating in individual and family therapy with me periodically for nearly two years. While Beth seeks out help from her teachers and her father (a mathematics maven), she was not receiving any official, outside school tutoring at the time of our interview. Her current grades fall primarily in the 'B' range."

"Laurence is a senior at a large suburban high school who graduates this spring and will be attending a state university to pursue an engineering degree. His diagnosis of Attention-Deficit/Hyperactivity Disorder, Combined Type occurred in second grade, along with the identification of his dyslexia and dysgraphia. Laurence attended a private school for children with learning disabilities in grades 3-8 before matriculating into a public high school for grades 9-12. As a result of his strong high school academic record, he has earned an academic scholarship to the university that he will be attending this fall."

Before and after medication: What's it like?

I asked Amy about the role stimulants had played in helping her manage in the school setting. "Before medication I remember not being able to comprehend what was going on in class because I couldn't focus. By that I mean, the moment something became too hard or too complex, I would zone out and then nothing stuck. Everyone else seemed to know what was going on and what the answers were. All of this made me  feel embarrassed as a young child because I thought I was stupid, which wiped out my confidence. After taking medication for a while and learning about my condition, I felt like I was finally able to participate in school because I was better able to control my ability to focus. That doesn't mean I suddenly could retain everything; it's not a genius medication. I'm still as confused as the rest of the class at times if the material is hard. But with medication, my mind is no longer left behind."

Beth struggled in middle school, particularly in science, math, English and Latin, and she recalled feeling particularly helpless during group instruction. I asked her about the class setting before and after receiving medication. "Without medication, it's just words going in one ear and out the other. Since you don't know that you have a real problem, it takes a  toll on your confidence, particularly when comparing yourself to other students and with what you think your own capabilities are academically. Since I've been taking medication, I'm much more engaged in classes and in teachers' lectures to the point where I'm able to follow and retain the information I'm receiving. It's fascinating if you've never been able to do it before. It's like opening a door to the other half of your abilities."

I also asked Beth, who has had both academic improvements and setbacks since starting therapy, how she thought the use of medication would impact her performance over time. "I definitely think that continuing to use medication will help my academic achievement in the long run. It's not even that you're learning more in your classes. It's that you are learning how to learn, per se. All the medicine does is allow you to bring your resources to bear like anyone else, but only if you want to."

I asked Laurence, who was challenged with both dyslexia and dysgraphia in addition to ADHD, what he remembered about his conditions prior to medication and how stimulants changed it. "My mom remembers when she would console me as a child, saying things along the lines of, 'You are smart; you just learn differently.' My response would be, 'How can I be smart when I can't read?' Everybody knew I was active and impulsive, but being that way wasn't that unusual. What came to the forefront was my

70

inability to read. In class, I could focus in for about five minutes each hour. This was really hard, because everyone was progressing faster than me. When I was placed on stimulant medication, I was able to concentrate on reading lessons in school and, because of that, I was able to do any homework by myself. My mom tells me that I became happier and my behavior improved. Before I was able to read, I was depressed and angry, and I was sulking around my house all the time."

I also asked Laurence what role stimulant medication has played in his learning how to compensate for his learning disabilities. "At my special school, I was taught strategies that allowed me to study efficiently and to do my homework consistently. Taking stimulant medication permits me the extended concentration I need to utilize the strategies I was taught. Stimulant medication is like the glue that holds all the other supports together."

Side effects: What are they?

All three agreed that adverse side effects of stimulant medication are manageable. Amy: "The only noticeable problem I have is I lose my appetite for an hour or two after taking my medication, but it doesn't affect my everyday life." Beth: "Stimulants make me a little more subdued, maybe a little loss of appetite, but that's not big. The benefits greatly outweigh the costs." Laurence: "They're manageable and worth the trade-off. I would be willing to suffer far worse side effects before I would stop taking stimulant medication."

Short-term benefits only? Would changes in environment yield as much or more?

Finally, I asked them what they would like to say to Dr. Sroufe, particularly regarding his central points that, at best, stimulants produce only short term benefits in achievement and behavior and that the development of ADHD is due more to environmental variables than any brain-based irregularities. Amy: "I agree with Dr. Sroufe's point that medication alone won't make a significant impact. Psychotherapy gave me knowledge about how ADHD affects me and how to control it, but the medication allowed me to take what I had learned and actually manage my ADHD effectively. Mainly, I'd tell Dr. Sroufe that by taking medication as a little child, I was able to realize that I wasn't stupid, but that I had ADHD. Learning that, and learning how to overcome its obstacles, helped me build confidence." Beth: "Based on my own experience, I cannot see environmental variables are the main reason for ADD. My school and home environments are close to ideal in terms of quality and support, and I still wasn't able to bring my resources to bear. It took getting the ADD diagnosis, taking stimulant medication and deciding to work hard in order for me to overcome the academic problems that I was having." Laurence: "I would tell him he is wrong. Without ten years of consistent stimulant medication along with good instruction, I would not be going to college on a full scholarship."

Conclusion: Necessary but not sufficient

In 2012, the conclusion I drew from Amy, Beth and Lawrence was that medication was a necessary but not sufficient condition for managing the impact of ADHD on their school achievement. Chief among the other "conditions" leading to success was the development of a personalized understanding of what ADHD is; regaining confidence in one's abilities and adopting mind sets and strategies that allow for effective compensation. I also thought that insights such as the ones they shared should be entered into the matrix of decision-making which shapes the development of large scale research studies. These first-hand accounts spawned a critical insight: that our thinking regarding stimulants and attention- deficit disorder must be informed not only by the conclusions of methodologically sound research, but also by the perspectives of patients providing compelling "data" which we would be foolish to omit, ignore or minimize.

Interviewee follow-up, 2014

I was curious as to how the interviewees' views about stimulants might change over time. In December 2014, Amy and Beth provided some additional comments about ADHD and stimulant medication.

In her follow-up, Amy commented on what she sees as her fellow students' misunderstanding about the nature of the condition and the role of medication to treat it: "The main thing that drives me nuts is that they think medication is only needed for school and the rest of the time people like me can function outside of academics. But in no way is that true. Lots of other life tasks are difficult to do without medication. Those comments really bother me because they so underestimate just how much difficulty I have all day long – starting a paper, cleaning up my room, organizing almost anything. Classmates also say, 'Oh yeah, I have trouble getting started too,' which seems like they are minimizing the extent of my problem."

Amy noted that one of her biggest challenges was "packing for an overnight trip." She also said that cleaning and organizing her room especially when the room is relatively full of possessions is also a problem. When she first got to college with a "blank slate" of a room to organize, the task was fairly easy to start. But as she said, "In my room at home or now my room at college, if the item doesn't have a particular spot to put it in, it takes me forever to decide. Shirts off hangers, where do they go? My drawers are full; where do I put these tee shirts. It's just like when I have to begin a paper, I don't know where to start. And I'm slightly a perfectionist, so I won't start something like a poster for a presentation until I have every piece of information. Medication doesn't fix all these decision-making and initiation problems, but at least with it, I'm less paralyzed."

Beth, now a college sophomore, reported that she had become particularly sensitive to and bothered by sweeping statements about ADHD and medication that were made not only by classmates but also by professionals on blogs or in articles she reads. She noted one article in which a mental health professional likened ADHD to a "mythical creature which we think we recognize but don't really know." Beth said that the same mental health professional went on to suggest that "stimulant medication wasn't needed." Beth finds such statements troubling, commenting: "My ADHD diagnosis did not occur until my freshman year of high school, and I have spent the better part of the last four years learning how to manage it through a combination of medication, psychotherapy and increasing my understanding about the nature of the condition and devising strategies to deal with it that work for me. Medication has played a big role in helping me to learn how to manage my ADHD, as have the other supports I've had. Comments from mental health professionals which cast doubt on its validity, despite decades of studies indicating that it is real, just make it more difficult to maintain the commitment to do the hard work required every day to manage ADHD effectively."

Interviewee follow-up, 2017

As I was finishing up the creation of this book, it seemed fitting to reach out to my interviewees one last time about what they have come to understand about ADHD and its management, and the role medication plays in that effort. Amy and Beth are now young adults. Amy graduated from college in 2016 and is pursuing specialty training to be a technician in a medical field. Beth will graduate from college in May 2018 and plans to pursue graduate study in psychology. Here are their thoughts:

Understanding and managing ADHD

Amy now sees an analogy between understanding and managing ADHD and learning how to drive. For her, psychotherapy, which helped her understand and devise compensations for the condition, was like earning her driver's license. There were certain competencies she had to have in order to be prepared to drive. Taking medication responsibly was analogous to owning and operating a car. As Amy put it, "you need both a license and experience operating a real car safely in order to be considered a qualified driver." Likewise, "to manage ADHD well, you have to have both the understanding (e.g., a license) and medication (e.g., operating a car) if you are really going to drive the condition and get somewhere you want to go."

Beth: "My advice to others working to manage their ADHD is to embrace your strengths and weaknesses. Over the years, it has helped me tremendously to get to know and position myself in a way that allows me to thrive. Something as little as realizing that you are most alert and productive in the morning can make a big difference. Maintaining perspective is very important for managing ADHD. In college I found profound strength in my passion for my major studies, and this helped me get through the required courses outside my major, which I found more challenging. It is easy to feel like a failure when you have a condition like ADHD. My advice is to cultivate positive self-talk, to appreciate yourself for your strengths and to understand that even though you will face sometimes daunting challenges, you are strong and capable."

The role of medication

Amy's recent job experience has helped to put medication into perspective for her. "I've been working recently in a place where holistic approaches are sometimes used or emphasized. While I don't doubt that holistic approaches may be helpful for ADHD, stimulant medication for me has been an essential component. Medication alone won't cure ADHD, ditto for psychotherapy. Using both approaches together is what has made the difference for me."

Beth: "In my case, medication is absolutely paramount to the long-term management of my ADHD. While I have had so much additional support from therapy, family and academic accommodations, medication ties everything together and maximizes the benefits of these supports. I truly believe that behavioral therapy and other forms of intervention are truly helpful and, quite frankly, necessary in many cases. But stimulant medication is the reason I have seen such dramatic change in my condition. I think of it this way: where medication addresses and compensates for the constitutional defects in my brain, behavioral therapy teaches me how to harness those benefits to compensate in everyday life."

On growing older

Amy: "I definitely think growing older helped with managing my ADHD, because I can see that it's now easier for me to do boring tasks that were more challenging for me to handle when I was younger. Some things are still hard, like holding onto information relayed to me verbally. With ADHD, I know I have to find the little tricks to help myself remember those things. A coworker can hold the information in memory, no problem. In the past, I might have fooled myself into thinking I could do that as well. Now I know that with my working memory issues, I need to write down the necessary information, and sometimes I ask to have it repeated."

Beth: "For an adolescent, the world revolves around him/her in a kind of tortuous, narrow way. Add ADHD to that mix and everything is intensified. The combination can lead you to have disdain for the world and its expectations, which can prevent you from achieving ultimately what you want in life. So with age and growth of executive functions, you have a greater opportunity to overcome the early limitations of ADHD. Again, it's easy to feel like a failure; to feel like the world wasn't built for your brain. It can make you bitter, but if you let go of that bitterness in your head and heart, you open up a space inside yourself to really grow."

Losing confidence

Amy: "This is no longer as much of an issue. At work, I don't feel judged. If I can't remember a doctor's instruction for a medication dose the first time it's given, and I have to ask for it again, that's okay. When I forget information, I'm just matter-of-fact about having missed it. What's most important is that I don't mess up my treatment and do something harmful. Some things have gotten easier. I know how to study effectively now, and I'm not afraid to be wrong. Absorbing new information that is quickly delivered verbally – that's still hard. But I know if I use a visual support, like making a list of things to remember, I do better. With ADHD, you have to use your strengths to help offset your weaknesses. And it's different for each person. Just because we have ADHD, it doesn't mean we don't have individual patterns of strengths and weaknesses."

Beth: "Now that I have embraced my weaknesses and recognize my strengths, I don't feel as though I need to apologize or explain myself to anyone. My colleague at work, who is a senior, is super-organized and great at managing the stages of long-term projects. She'll occasionally provide comments like, 'Have you done this yet?' 'Have you started that?' The implication is that her management style is superior, but that doesn't work for me. It's not that I'm not going finish whatever needs to be done; it's just that I have a different process. For example, it may take me a little longer to build my motivation, but once I have it, the quality of my work is excellent and it's done on time."

"I've come to a balance point between doing things my own way and adapting to expectations of the outside world. My confidence doesn't suffer because I now know how to be productive in my own way and on my own terms."

Medication is only one layer in building a firm foundation for change

Laurence commented that stimulant medication is "the glue that holds all supports together," which is true, but the impact is even greater than just holding things together. What I've learned from the three interviewees and others in my practice is that the medication can be transformative in terms of helping individuals understand how their executive functions operate; where the shortcomings lie; and what they need to do to compensate. Many times, the awareness of how one's executive functions operate emerges slowly and only with some fairly deep reflection about the before-and-after change.

Listen to the comments of Liz, a 56-year-old mother and homemaker who struggled with this condition for most of her life. She was the eldest person on whom I have done an initial evaluation. After two plus years of medication therapy and actively managing the condition, here is what she had to say about the role of medication. "I'm not who I want to be or who I am when I'm not taking medication. When my dose was too low, I noticed it. I was snapping (easily annoyed) at people; I was interrupting others who were speaking to me; my motivation was declining; and I wasn't having control over my appetite and eating. I was seeing myself losing ground."

And we end with the reflections of James, 65, a husband and father of a son and daughter, both adults, one of whom has ADHD. In adulthood, James was identified as having the predominantly inattentive form of the condition and he takes stimulant medication primarily during the work week. Career reversals forced him to examine his executive functions, particularly related to his work roles. Here is what he has to say about the nature of ADHD. "While I have had this condition for years, I don't think it's really a problem with attention. I'm rarely distracted from specific tasks; in fact, I can become over-focused on a particular task to the detriment of other things that I need to get done. In many cases, those other tasks can be more critical to overall job performance. I think this form of ADHD is more properly called 'meta-inattentive type.' My issue is maintaining attention to multiple tasks and timelines, as well as the feedback that I receive from co-workers and clients. I found that stimulant medication helps me to broaden my focus while not compromising my attention to individual tasks."

CHAPTER 6
Pulling it all together

Welcome to the end of the book and thank you for staying the course with me. I hope the reward for your effort is a deeper understanding about what ADHD is and how best to manage it. By now you can also empathize with the frustration and concern I had in late 2012 having read newspaper articles that didn't capture accurately the condition or the treatment. In fairness to the media, though, how could it really be otherwise? To grasp the full measure of ADHD's influence, there is a lot to learn. For starters, we need to understand the nature of executive functions -- how they are responsible for guiding and directing behavior. Add to that the need to know how ADHD disrupts the smooth development and operation of executive functions, a process that begins in infancy and may extend into early adulthood or even throughout one's life.

By now I trust you understand the problem in thinking about the condition as just a collection of symptoms. The reality is that ADHD is bigger than that. So should a friend or family member speak to you about specific ADHD symptoms, I hope the "scope problem" previously discussed will flash in your mind, reminding you that more often than not, ADHD symptoms are neither circumscribed nor temporary. You may also recall how other factors (development, environmental structure and severity of the condition) influence how ADHD affects a particular person. Individuals with apparently similar diagnoses can vary widely as to how their day-to-day functioning is impacted. This is especially true for individuals with milder forms of the condition.

We covered three elements necessary to manage ADHD: behavior change, family dynamics and medication. For behavior change, target goals and behavior charts are essential ingredients, but I've found that these tools are only effective when they include self-evaluation and a way to receive feedback from others about task execution. Why? Because self-evaluation and incorporating feedback are usually lacking for individuals with ADHD.

My IM Self-Monitoring system is intended to help an individual work towards greater independence and improved quality of task execution because immediate feedback is provided through a metric (2,1,0). We also talked about developing an antecedent mindset as a way of getting organized in order to get out in front of one's actions. And when unproductive exchanges begin to escalate, there are approaches like STOP that help the individual who has trouble inhibiting to pause and arrest their actions.

In the area of family dynamics, understanding how ADHD can impact each family member's autonomy may help parents and children navigate better the constant challenges posed by ADHD. And given the high heritability of ADHD, parents must also be aware of potential challenges with their own behavior regulation. Given this, it's essential to define the obstacles to smooth family functioning clearly and non-judgmentally, and to get everyone to engage in coordinated teamwork to handle the challenges with behavior regulation that are manifest throughout the day.

As to medication, the perspectives of some of my patients make clear that if tolerated well, the benefits of improved inhibition, staying power and sustained engagement with tasks make handling life's responsibilities (academic, social, occupational) that much easier. At the same time, however, medication alone cannot, and will not, confer the full understanding of the condition, nor the wherewithal to manage it. That is something the individual must develop on their own with the support of loved ones.

It seems fitting to end the book with one last perspective. This one is from a mother Anna and her husband Daniel. They have two children with ADHD, Jennifer, age 9, and Danny, age 11. Jennifer has associated learning disabilities with prominent symptoms of hyperactivity/impulsivity and inattention, while Danny shows prominent symptoms of inattention. At the time, the family was relatively new to my practice, and both parents were in the throes of navigating a steep learning curve about what ADHD is and how to manage it. Over the course of back-to-back school meetings for each child, which Anna described as a "marathon," she essentially made the same case for each child.

"Daniel and I want our children to receive the support they need in learning how to handle their ADHD day-by-day. We see, though, that it has got to be the right kind of support, the kind that provides understanding about how difficult it is for them to make and maintain behavior changes, but also the kind that doesn't let them off the hook about finding (sometimes by unpleasant consequences) what they need to do to manage it. It's a matter of finding the balance between those two goals when you are dealing with a condition that has such a big impact every day."

While Anna and her family continue to wrestle with understanding and managing ADHD effectively, her comments over the course of that morning embody what I hope will transpire for all families. It is this: that they develop a working understanding of this condition and its management, while at the same time remaining proactive and optimistic about what is possible.

Acknowledgments

Had it not been for the encouragement, collaboration and devotion of many people, this book would never have been written. Interestingly, the range of contributors is broad – newspaper and free-lance editors, mental health professionals, educators, artists, patients and their families, and even my own family.

First in line is Sue Mermelstein, Letters Editor at *The New York Times,* who played a major role in selecting my letters for publication, edited initial drafts of the book, and provided unwavering encouragement. Virginia Smith did a splendid job editing the later versions of the book and navigating the challenges of reviewing a book with cartoons. Penny Moldofsky provided useful suggestions that made the content more engaging and readable. Thanks also to Pat Manley and Adrielle Munger for their comments and suggestions.

Bob Perkins' cartoons were created with care, patience and close attention to the text. He is a master at conveying emotions with touches of lightness and fun, and his technical abilities are nothing short of amazing. His former art teacher and mentor, Marion Kassab, collaborated with Bob, providing invaluable guidance and feedback to both of us. Thanks also to Ceily Perkins, Bob's mother, for providing transportation and encouragement all the way through the process.

Educators at local private schools for students with learning disabilities also endorsed the project. They are William Keeney (Delaware Valley Friends School), Penny Moldofsky (Woodlynde School), Marion Kassab and Thomas Needham (Hill Top Preparatory School). Additionally, Martha Biery (reading specialist at Child Study Institute, Bryn Mawr College) provided valuable suggestions.

My mental health colleagues are the "best," always cheering me on. Thanks to psychologists Grace Ashton, Carole Bogdanoff, Marisa Crandall, Eugenie Flaherty, Julie Faude, Ann Gluck, Peter Wiley and Anne Robbins, and to psychiatrists C. Pace Duckett, Manely Ghaffari, Jeffrey Naser, Terry Peura (CRNP in Dr. Naser's office), Amy Rowan and Anthony Rostain, who also helped co-write an op-ed article with me. I would be remiss if I didn't mention two psychologists whose examples have had a lasting impact on the work that I do -- my dissertation advisor at Bryn Mawr College, the late Janet L. Hoopes, and my training director at Philadelphia Child Guidance Clinic, David Abelsohn.

Thanks to all my patients and their families, past and present, who have allowed me to develop the Integrated Model and refine the thinking that underpins it.

Finally, my children, Matthew and Carrie, endured what must have seemed like endless conversations about the book. Matt provided unfailing encouragement, and Carrie added editorial and IT support. My sister, Ellen Coolidge, also provided unfailing encouragement and even paid some of the outside editorial expenses. Last and most significantly is my husband Bill who typed, edited, listened, tolerated bouts of irritability and insecurity, and never stopped believing in me.

Appendices

APPENDIX 1

Barkley's Hybrid Model of Executive Functions

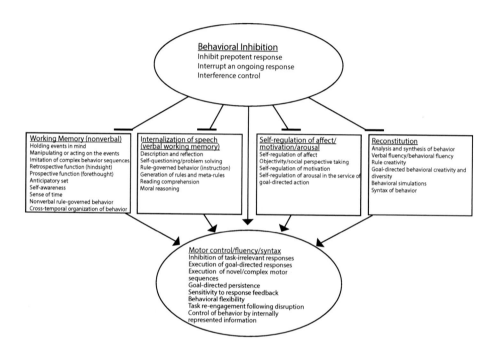

FIGURE 7.7 The complete hybrid model of executive functiones (boxes) and the relationship of these four functions to the behavvioral inhibition and motor control systems.

Source: Barkley, R.A. (1997) *ADHD and the nature of self-control.* New York: Guilford Press. p. 191. (Reprinted with permission of Guilford Press.)

The diagram on page 21 is my adaptation of Barkley's hybrid model of executive functions, which is shown above. I developed it for teaching purposes only.

APPENDIX 2

Diagnostic & Statistical Manual of Mental Disorders, Fifth Edition: Diagnostic Criteria for Attention-Deficit/Hyperactivity Disorder (ADHD)

A. A persistent pattern of inattention and/or hyperactivity that interferes with functioning or development characterized by (1) and/or (2):

1. **Inattention:** Six (or more) of the following symptoms have persisted for at least 6 months to a degree that is inconsistent with developmental level and that negatively impacts directly on social and academic/occupational activities:

Note: The symptoms are not solely a manifestation of oppositional behavior, defiance, hostility, or failure to understand task instructions.) For older adolescents and adults (age 17 and older), at least five symptoms are required.

   a. Often fails to give close attention to details or makes careless mistakes in schoolwork, at work, or during other activities (e.g., overlooks or misses details, work is inaccurate).

   b. Often has difficulty sustaining attention in tasks or play activities (e.g., has difficulty remaining focused during lectures, conversations, or lengthy reading).

   c. Often does not seem to listen when spoken to directly (e.g., mind seems elsewhere, even in the absence of any obvious distraction).

   d. Often does not follow through on instructions and fails to finish schoolwork, chores, or duties in the workplace (e.g., starts tasks but quickly loses focus and is easily sidetracked).

   e. Often has difficulty organizing tasks and activities (e.g., difficulty managing sequential tasks; difficulty keeping materials and belongings in order; messy, disorganized work; has poor time management; fails to meet deadlines).

   f. Often avoids, dislikes, or is reluctant to engage in tasks that require sustained mental effort (e.g., schoolwork or homework; for older adolescents and adults, preparing reports, completing forms, reviewing lengthy papers).

   g. Often loses things necessary for tasks or activities (e.g., school materials, pencils, books, tools, wallets, keys, paperwork, eyeglasses, mobile telephones).

   h. Is often easily distracted by extraneous stimuli (for older adolescents and adults, may include unrelated thoughts).

   i. Is often forgetful in daily activities (e.g., doing chores, running errands; for older adolescents and adults, returning calls, paying bills, keeping appointments).

2. **Hyperactivity and impulsivity:** Six (or more) of the following symptoms have persisted for at least 6 months to a degree that is inconsistent with developmental level and that negatively impacts directly on social and academic/occupational activities:

Note: The symptoms are not solely a manifestation of oppositional behavior, defiance, hostility, or failure to understand task instructions. For older adolescents and adults (age 17 and older), at least five symptoms are required.

a. Often fidgets with or taps with hands or feet or squirms in seat.

b. Often leaves seat situations where remaining seated is expected (e.g., leaves his or her place in the classroom, in the office or other workplace, or in other situations that require remaining in place).

c. Often runs about or climbs in situations where it is inappropriate. (**Note:** In adolescents or adults, may be limited to feeling restless).

d. Often unable to play or engage in leisure activities quietly.

e. Is often "on the go," acting as if "driven by a motor" (e.g., is unable to be or uncomfortable being still for extended time, as in restaurants, meetings; may be experienced by others as being restless or difficult to keep up with).

f. Often talks excessively.

g. Often blurts out an answer before a question has been completed (e.g., completes people's sentences; cannot wait for turn in conversation).

h. Often has difficulty waiting his or her turn (e.g., while waiting in line).

i. Often interrupts or intrudes on others (e.g., butts into conversations, games, or activities; may start using other people's things without asking or receiving permission; for adolescents and adults, may intrude into or take over what others are doing).

B. Several hyperactive-impulsive or inattentive symptoms were present prior to age 12 years.

C. Several inattentive or hyperactive-impulsive symptoms are present in two or more settings (e.g., at home, school, or work; with friends or relatives; in other activities).

D. There is clear evidence that the symptoms interfere with, or reduce the quality of, social, academic, or occupational functioning.

E. The symptoms do not occur exclusively during the course of schizophrenia or another psychotic disorder and are not better explained by another mental disorder (e.g., mood disorder, anxiety disorder, dissociative disorder, personality disorder, substance intoxication or withdrawal).

Specify whether:

314.01 (F90.2) Combined presentation: If both Criteria Al (inattention) and A2 (hyperactivity-impulsivity) are met for the past 6 months.

314.00 (F90.0) Predominantly inattentive presentation: If Criterion Al (inattention) is met but Criterion A2 (hyperactivity-impulsivity) is not met for the past 6 months.

314.01 (F90.1) Predominantly hyperactive-impulsive presentation: If Criterion A2 (hyperactivity-impulsivity) is met but Criterion Al (inattention) is not met for the past 6 months.

Specify if:

In partial remission: When full criteria were previously met, fewer than the full criteria have been met for the past 6 months, and the symptoms still result in impairment in social, academic, or occupational functioning.

Specify current severity:

Mild: Few, if any, symptoms in excess of those required to make the diagnosis are present, and symptoms result in no more than minor impairment in social or occupational functioning.

Moderate: Symptoms or functional impairment between "mild" and "severe" are present.

Severe: Many symptoms in excess of those required to make the diagnosis, or several symptoms that are particularly severe, are present, or the symptoms result in marked impairment in social or occupational functioning.

References

Author's Note

Cohen, P. & Rasmussen, N. (2013, June 16). A nation of kids on speed. *The Wall Street Journal.* Retrieved from http://online.wsj.com/article

Hruska, B. (2012, August 18). Raising the Ritalin generation. *The New York Times.* Retrieved from http://www.nytimes.com

Ratey, J.J. with Hagerman, E. (2008). *Spark: The revolutionary new science of exercise and the brain.* New York: Little Brown & Company.

Schwartz, C. (2017, October 16). Generation Adderall. *The New York Times Magazine,* Retrieved from http://www.nytimes.com

Schwarz, A. (2012, October 9). Attention disorder or not, pills to help in school. *The New York Times.* Retrieved from http://www.nytimes.com

Schwarz, A. (2012, June 10). Risky rise of the good grade pill. *The New York Times.* Retrieved from http://www.nytimes.com

Schwarz, A. (2013, February 2). Drowned in a stream of prescriptions. *The New York Times.* Retrieved from http://www.nytimes.com

Sroufe, L.A. (2012, January 28). Ritalin gone wrong. *The New York Times.* Retrieved from http://nytimes.com

Sutherland, F.C. (2016, October 30). [Letter to the editor in response to Schwartz, C. (2017, October 16)]. Generation Adderall, *The New York Times Magazine,* p. 12.

Sutherland, F.C. (2012, October 5). *Management of ADHD: An integrated model of theory and practice.* Presentation at the annual conference of the Philadelphia branch of the International Dyslexia Association, Stratford, PA.

Sutherland, F.C. (2012, June 12). [Letter to the editor in response to Schwarz, A. (2012, June 10)]. Risky rise of the good grade pill. *The New York Times,* p. A22.

Sutherland, F.C. (2012, December 5). Invitation to a dialogue: How to treat ADHD. *The New York Times,* p. A24.

Sutherland, F.C. (2012, December 9). Sunday Dialogue: Medicating for ADHD. *The New York Times*, p. SR2.

Sutherland, F.C. (2013, April 30). [Letter to the editor in response to Thakkar, V.G. (2013, April 28)]. Diagnosing the wrong deficit. *The New York Times*, p. A16.

Sutherland, F.C. (2012). *Stimulants and attention-deficit disorder: Three perspectives.* Unpublished article.

Sutherland, F.C. & Rostain, A.L. (2013). *A false dichotomy: Excluding parents in the mental health treatment of their young adult offspring.* Unpublished article.

Thakkar, V.G. (2013, April 28). Diagnosing the wrong deficit. *The New York Times*, pp. SR1, SR6.

Chapter 1

Biederman, J., Faraone, S.V., Mick, E., Spencer, T., Wilens, T., Kiely, K., et al. (1995). High risk for attention deficit hyperactivity disorder among children of parents with childhood onset of the disorder: A pilot study. *American Journal of Psychiatry, 152,* 431-435.

American Psychiatric Association (2013). *Diagnostic and statistical manual of mental disorders (5th ed.).* Arlington, VA: Author.

Chapter 2

Books:

Barkley, R.A. (1997). *ADHD and the nature of self-control.* New York: Guilford Press.

Barkley, R.A. (1998). *Attention-deficit hyperactivity disorder: A handbook for diagnosis and treatment (2nd ed.).* New York: Guilford Press.

Barkley, R.A. (2012). *Executive functions: What they are, how they work and why they evolved.* New York: Guilford Press.

Barkley, R.A. (Ed.) (2015). *Attention-deficit hyperactivity disorder: A handbook for diagnosis and treatment (4th ed.).* New York: Guilford Press.

Dawson, P. & Guare, R. (2004). *Executive skills in children and adolescents: A practical guide to assessment and intervention.* New York: Guilford Press.

Weiss, G. & Hechtman, L.T. (1993). *Hyperactive children grown up: ADHD in children, adolescents and adults (2nd ed.).* New York: Guilford Press.

Wender, P.H. (1995). *Attention-deficit hyperactivity disorder in adults.* New York: Oxford University Press.

Chapters and Studies:

Baddeley, A. (1992). Working memory. *Science, 255,* 556-559.

Baddeley, A.D. & Hitch, G.J. (1994). Developments in the concept of working memory. *Neuropsychology, 8,* 485-493.

Barkley, R.A., DuPaul, G.J., & McMurray, M.B. (1990). A comprehensive evaluation of attention deficit disorder with and without hyperactivity. *Journal of Consulting and Clinical Psychology, 58,* 775-789.

Diamond, A. (2013). Executive functions. *Annual Review of Psychology, 64,* 135-168.

Diamond, A. (2006). The development of executive functions. In E. Bialystock & F.I.M. Craik (Eds.) *Lifespan cognition: Mechanisms of change* (pp. 70-95). New York: Oxford University Press.

Diamond, A. (2005). Attention-deficit disorder (attention-deficit/hyperactivity disorder without hyperactivity): A neurobiologically and behaviorally distinct disorder from attention-deficit/hyperactivity disorder (with hyperactivity). *Development and Psychopathology, 17,* 807-825.

Douglas, V. (1983). Attention and cognitive problems. In M. Rutter (Ed) *Developmental neuropsychiatry* (pp. 280-329). New York: Guilford Press.

Hitch, G.J. (2006). Working memory in children: a cognitive approach. In E. Bialystock & F.I.M. Craik (Eds.) *Lifespan cognition: Mechanisms of change.* (pp. 112-127). New York: Oxford University Press.

Chapter 3

Braswell, L. & Bloomquist, M.L. (1991). *Cognitive-behavioral therapy with ADHD children: Child, family and school interventions.* New York: Guilford Press.

Furth, H.G. (1981). *Piaget and knowledge: Theoretical foundations (2nd ed.).* Chicago, IL: University of Chicago Press.

Ginsburg, H. & Opper S. (1979). *Piaget's theory of intellectual development (2nd ed.).* Englewood Cliffs, NJ: Prentice-Hall, Inc.

Piaget, J. & Inhelder, B. (1958). *The growth of logical thinking from childhood to adolescence.* (A. Parsons & S. Seagram, Trans.) New York: Basic Books, Inc.

Piaget, J. & Inhelder, B. (1964). *The early growth of logic in the child.* (E.A. Lunzer & D. Papert, Trans.) London, England: Routledge and Kegan Paul, Ltd.

Stein, J. & Urdang, L. (Eds.) (1967). *The random house dictionary of the english language. The unabridged edition.* New York: Random House.

Skinner, B.F. (1966). What is the experimental analysis of behavior? *Journal of the Experimental Analysis of Behavior, 9,* 213-218.

Sutherland, F.C. (2008). *IM self-monitoring and stop strategy.* Unpublished text in Power Point presentation.

Chapter 4

Erikson, E.H. (1963). *Childhood and society (2nd ed.).* New York: W.W. Norton & Co.

Freud, S. (1966). General theory of the neuroses. In J. Strachey (Ed and Trans.) *Introductory lectures on psychoanalysis: The standard edition* (pp 243-463). New York: WW Norton & Company. (Original work published in 1917).

Hall, C.S. & Lindzey, G. (1970). *Theories of personality (2nd ed.).* New York: John Wiley & Sons, 29-77.

Minuchin, S. (1974). *Families & family therapy.* Cambridge, MA: Harvard University Press.

Minuchin, S. & Fishman, H.C. (1981). *Family therapy techniques.* Cambridge, MA: Harvard University Press.

Chapter 5

Sroufe, L.A. (2012, January 28). Ritalin gone wrong. *The New York Times,* Retrieved from http://www.nytimes.com

List of Resources

Barkley, R.A. (2013). *Taking charge of ADHD: The complete, authoritative guide for parents (3rd ed.).* New York: Guilford Press.

Barkley, R.A., Murphy, K.R. & Fischer, M. (2008). *ADHD in adults: What the science says.* New York: Guilford Press.

Murphy, K.R. & LeVert, S. (1995). *Out of the fog: Treatment options and coping strategies for adult attention deficit disorder.* New York: Hyperion.

Wilens, T.E. and Hammerness, P.G. (2016). *Straight talk about psychiatric medications for kids (4th ed.).* New York: Guilford Press.

About the Author

Frances C. Sutherland is a clinical-developmental psychologist who specializes in the adjustment problems associated with ADHD, learning disabilities and related mental health issues. Working with children, adolescents, adults and their families, Dr. Sutherland has more than 25 years of experience in private practice. She has developed the Integrated Model of ADHD Management and has given presentations on the topic of ADHD to professionals, parents and general audiences. In the past six years, her letters to the *New York Times* on the subject of ADHD have been published in the *Letters* section and in the *Thread,* the letters section of the *Sunday Magazine.* In late 2012, one of her letters was the basis for an editorial feature article, *Sunday Dialogue.*

About the Illustrator

Bob Perkins is a free-lance illustrator who specializes in creating cartoons. In addition to his work with Dr. Sutherland, he is developing a comic book, *The Misfits,* which tracks the adventures of young people with neurodevelopmental delays who are grappling with life's myriad challenges.

27428475R00053